BI
HEART

What people are saying

This book is enormous fun to read. But don't be deceived, the content of the message is about as profound as anything you will come across. The generous love of the God who 'did not withold his own Son but gave him up for us all' needs to be reflected by an equally generous church. Most of the Christians I have met get somewhere near this but just occasionally I meet those who if they have been baptised at all seem to have been baptised in lemon-juice! This book will do us all good and will push us in the right direction.

Dr Nigel G. Wright, Principal, Spurgeon's College London

Congratulations, Chris Duffett and Simon Goddard, for your creativity in giving a title to the book. Yes, it caught my attention right away, but I must confess that it did not ring a bell that I would be reading about Evangelism.

And yet, as I now look back at the book, there I find Evangelism defined in a very straightforward way – Big-hearted, the gospel of simple words and a large heart. Interestingly, Chris and Simon offer a blunt heads-up about the content of the book in the preamble by telling the reader what he or she is about to read without any effort to disguise or pretend that Evangelism is just an "in passing" idea contained somewhere in the book. No, Evangelism is what the book is all about! And so you and I are challenged to live our daily

Christian life with the heart-gripping conviction that a big-hearted God provides us with a big-hearted gospel and expects us as churches and individual Christians to be characterized by a big-hearted compassion and big-hearted innovative approaches.
Fausto A. Vasconcelos, Director, Division on Mission, Evangelism & Theological Reflection Baptist World Alliance

This book is for anyone whose heart longs to share Jesus with others, but whose head has warned 'don't' . Chris and Simon show us how we can have a creative partnership with God, using the gifts we have already, to be effective big-hearted missionaries right where we are.
The Revd Kathryn Morgan, Mission Advisor Baptist Union

Chris and Simon write from their everyday experiences of what God can do and how he does it through very ordinary people. Evangelism is not a popular word today but these writers will help you look at what it means to be involved in Gods mission to his world. This book will impact not simply your head but also your heart and your actions. If you want to be involved in Gods adventure of faith make sure you read this and then get going.
Dave Male, Director of the Centre for Pioneer Learning Cambridge

Chris writes with great passion about our loving heavenly Father, reminding us of what a big-hearted God He really is. As you read this book, you will travel to the place Jesus wants you to be, doing, sharing, loving, involving and living the good news of the Gospels, all together in His very inclusive Kingdom.

Throughout this book you will find encouraging examples and testimonies that will empower you to get up and 'do something'.
Simon's section on Big Hearted Church brings a fresh new model of church to both 'in and out' the building. He shows us how 'do church' everywhere we are and in everything we do.

This book is written in an easy-to-read style. Its content is so relevant to every church member, church leader, Christians in

general and even readers totally unfamiliar with Christianity. It captures the very essence of how amazingly great the Father's love is for us. I really enjoyed every aspect of the book.
Rev Denise Evangelista DeOliveira, Assistant Pastor Greenford Baptist Church

Big Hearted challenges the reader to stop simply talking about it, to stop running away from it... and to just get on with the evangelistic task of making Jesus known! Chris & Simon do this in a warm-hearted, accessible way, with good humour and passionate conviction. Buy it for your leadership team and decide to act!
Jez Brown, Regional Minister South West Baptist Association

In these days of 3D movies Chris and Simon give us a vision of a 3D Christian and a 3D church. To be Big Hearted is to be someone who is living and sharing the Christian faith in full 3D.
Andy Glover, Hoole Baptist Church

The apparently simple approach Chris has to making God's love real is of course deceptively deep. It reaches way into our humanity, touching parts of us we'd long forgotten were there. This book is, in the very best sense, a treasury of encouragement and love.
Mark Craig, BMS World Mission Director for Communications

Refreshing, Exciting, Stretching, Terrifying, Arresting, Revealing, Inspiring, and so much more... what Chris and Simon have tapped into is, I believe, a fresh breath of the Spirit of God releasing to the church not just creative but vibrantly beautiful expressions of the Father's heart. This is a book for the moment and also one that should inspire generations to follow in their wake. You won't be able to think about evangelism in the same way after you've read it - there, I did try and warn you!
Jonathan Vaughan-Davies, Bethel Baptist Church Whitchurch

BIG HEARTED

The gospel of simple words and a large heart

Chris Duffett &
Simon Goddard

GILEAD
B O O K S

Gilead Books Publishing
Corner Farm
West Knapton
Malton
North Yorkshire YO17 8JB UK
www.GileadBooksPublishing.com

First published in Great Britain, May 2012
Reprinted July 2012
2 4 6 8 10 9 7 5 3

Copyright © Chris Duffett & Simon Goddard 2012

British Library Cataloguing-in-Publication Data:
A catalogue record for this book is available from the British Library.

ISBN-13: 978-0-9568560-5-0

All rights reserved.
No part of this publication may be reproduced, stored in a retrieval system or
transmitted in any form or by any means, electronic, mechanical, photocopying,
recording or otherwise, without the prior permission of the publisher.

All scripture quotations, unless otherwise indicated, are taken from the HOLY BIBLE,
NEW INTERNATIONAL VERSION. Copyright © 1973, 1978, 1984 by International
Bible Society. Used by permission of Hodder & Stoughton, a member of the Hodder
Headline Group. All rights reserved. 'NIV' is a trademark of International Bible
Society. UK trademark number 1448790.

Scripture quotations marked (TNIV) are taken from the HOLY BIBLE, TODAY'S NEW
INTERNATIONAL VERSION®. TNIV®. Copyright © 2001, 2005 by International
Bible Society. Used by permission of Zondervan. All rights reserved.

Scripture quotations marked (CEV) are from the Contemporary English Version
Copyright © 1991, 1992, 1995 by American Bible Society, Used by Permission.

Scripture quotations marked (The Message) are taken from The Message. Copyright
©1993, 1994, 1995, 1996, 2000, 2001, 2002. Used by permission of NavPress
Publishing Group.

Scripture quotations marked (NKJV) are taken from the New King James Version.
Copyright © 1982 by Thomas Nelson Inc. Used by permission. All rights reserved.

The publisher makes every effort to ensure that the papers used in our books are
made from trees that have been legally sourced from well-managed and credibly
certified forests by using a printer awarded FSC & PEFC chain of custody
certification.

Dedications

Chris dedicates this book to
Milly and Beatrice.
His beautiful big-hearted girls.

Simon dedicates this book to
his wonderful wife, Lisa.

Acknowledgements

Chris writes: I've read a few acknowledgements in books recently where the opening sentence is something on the lines of, 'They say it takes a village to raise a baby, just so with this book...' and as predictable and as cheesy as it may sound I too want to humbly acknowledge that this book is a team effort which has been birthed and dragged up by an amazing bunch of people who make up my village, albeit you're all over the UK.

First and foremost thank you to my beautiful wife who patiently puts up with my spontaneity and lack of 9-5 routine, the way you cope with my mad entrepreneur ideas of getting the gospel 'out there' with such big-hearted support is amazing! Thank you so much to my children Seth, Beatrice and Milly who teach me so much and who sometimes miss out on Daddy time as I go to those who don't know Jesus. You three make me so proud.

Thank you also to all The Light Project team, you're passion for letting others get what we've got is inspirational. Especially thanks to the big-hearted Glyn Jones who helped me with some of the ideas in this book. I also want to thank my big Baptist Union family for the opportunities you have given me to serve you as an evangelist. Thank you also to those who serve with me in evangelism. The time you give and willingness to shine Jesus is amazing!

I want to make special mention of my pastor Phil Campion and our church family at Biggleswade Baptist Church, you are a great encouragement to me. Thank you to the blokes who pray for me when I send out texts and ask for support. I am also constantly encouraged by Dev Kruck who prays for me.

Lastly, thank you to those who have made this book a book: The thorough Sheena Fisher who edited it, and without whom spelling mistakes and typo's would be somewhat common place. The ever so clever and creative Richard Coan who designed the cover. The risk-taking publisher extraordinaire Chris Hayes of Gilead Books who once more has been willing to take another gamble on a fresh-faced writer with a heart for good news. Simon for writing this with me, your section is just superb and you're quite the example of being big-hearted. Thank you for those of you who had a sneak peak and gave some lovely comments about this book. To be really honest, your comments blew me away and gave me such confidence that the message in this book is one that needs to be shared. Also to John Drane for his insightful and challenging foreword, humbling to have a foreword from you, thank you. Lastly, to my heavenly father who loves me. I want you to know that I love you too.

Simon writes: I praise God for his love for me, and for the invitation to participate with him in his big-hearted mission. I want to thank Chris for giving me the opportunity to share our church's story and the lessons we have learnt over the last few years. I also want to recognise the generous spirit of those at RE:NEW, and to commend their willingness to leave the familiar and safe and follow God on the exciting and sometimes scary journey he's taken us on. It is important also to acknowledge the support that we've received from the wider church family – especially the local parish churches and the Baptists who contributed to the Home Mission grants that have made this ministry possible.

Finally I want to thank those who have encouraged and invested in me personally: my family and friends, the regional ministry team of the Eastern Baptist Association, the students and staff at Spurgeon's College, the fellowship at Zion Baptist Church in Cambridge who first recognised God's call upon my life, and, of course, my wonderful wife, Lisa, to whom I dedicate this book.

Foreword

I don't get to write many forewords for other people's books, so it's a particular privilege for me to be commending this one here. The topic that Chris and Simon tackle is one that has been close to the heart of my ministry for the best part of thirty years, as I've engaged in grass-roots missional activities as well as national and international strategic conversations with Christians of diverse persuasions and in many different countries. Yet for a lot of Christians, faith sharing has a bad image. It's something you wouldn't do to your dog, let alone someone whose friendship you valued. Chris and Simon tackle both the urgency and the reticence by starting in exactly the right place: with God. If God is the sort of angry tyrant that some seem to think, whose sole ambition is to put people down – even waging war against them – then it's hardly surprising that most people would find it hard to recognize that as any sort of good news. Thankfully, the model given to us by the life and teaching of Jesus (who for the Christian was and is the most authentic image of God) is rather different. Admittedly, he did get a bit steamed up now and again, but it's worth noting that the only people he ever got angry with were self-righteous religious types who thought they knew better than him. They were both irritated and surprised by Jesus' insistence that God is best understood not as an angry monster but as the shepherd who goes in search of the lost sheep, or the parent who cares deeply for a wayward child.

Not only does that challenge some commonly held images of God, but it also changes our understanding of mission. Too often, mission has been regarded as a good turn that reluctant Christians need to be persuaded to do to assist an otherwise helpless deity. But the reality is that God is already deeply involved in mission (that's what the incarnation is all about), and the true calling of the disciple is to recognize what God is doing and to get alongside that. The trouble is that God keeps doing things that some Christians are inclined to disapprove of – and so (in one of the many stories in this book) Chris and Simon find themselves in places like Greggs the bakers at a time on Sunday mornings when others think they should have been in church.

Stories like that highlight the big challenge facing Christians in today's world. At one time it would have been possible to invite people into church services, and they would have come. A few still do, but the majority would never dream of it, not because they're not spiritually concerned but, as it's been put to me many times "if we wanted to follow Jesus, we wouldn't do it that way". And "that way" is all too often the very things that we think will actually make our churches more attractive to outsiders. If we took more seriously the concerns of those who are searching for meaning in our increasingly fragmented culture, we might be surprised at how few of them appreciate the soft rock music that now seems to define the nature of worship, and how many of them are longing for meaningful prayer and other traditional forms of Christian devotion that have been marginalized in the effort to make churches seem trendy.

If instead of starting with the preferences of Christians, we were to start with what God is already doing in the world, I suspect we would come up with something rather different than what we have now, whether that be worship, ministry, or mission. It would be radical in the fundamental sense of the word (going back to the roots) but for that very reason would be more deeply connected to the ancient traditions of Christian spirituality and lifestyle. Seventy years ago, Archbishop William Temple said something about the church needing to be for the benefit of those who are not yet a part of it, and that is still the case today: we need to think less of the church and more about people, which is another way of saying with Jesus that we should be thinking more about others and less of ourselves. One reason that mission has become an optional extra for enthusiasts who are interested in that sort of thing is that many good and faithful believers spend all their energy servicing the institution and have no time left to connect with the rest of the world. Not that we can do without institutions. You would imagine that people in independent congregations would have more freedom to experiment, but paradoxically they can end up with less opportunity for creative missional engagement precisely because they lack the infrastructure of a well run institution, that can offer support as well as inspirational trans-local leadership.

These themes, and more, all surface in different ways here, which makes this quite a challenging book for some – though its combination of Biblical commonsense and personal stories will also be encouraging for others. The reality is that things not only are changing, but they have changed – in all churches of all theological and ecclesial shapes and sizes. The real question for us today is not whether our churches will change, but whether in the midst of the change that is already happening we are prepared to be the agents of intentional transformation. If we fail to take the initiative then we can be sure that we will be overtaken by changes that are random and unplanned, and will reflect whatever ideas happen to be trendy at any given moment. On the other hand, if we actively work for change (and a willingness to change is, after all, at the heart of the message of Jesus), then we can work to ensure that what happens next is in tune with what God is already doing. This book will be an invaluable inspiration in that endeavour – though for church life as it now is, it needs to carry a health warning!

John Drane

Contents

Getting it out in the open. Phew...

Let's do away with pleasantries. I'm getting down to business on the first page and I'm going to tell you what this book is about. Yep, I sure am. But, I must admit I'm nervous. You see, you may not like it. It may upset you or make you feel guilty or icky or itchy or like you need a stiff drink. Alternatively, you may think I'm some kind of weirdo harping on about some confusing subject. Yet I'm still going to tell you.

Okay, here goes: this book is about ... evangelism. There! I've done it and I realise that some of you will now be tempted to assign this book swiftly to that special shelf where other "interesting topic" or "well meaning, but not for me" or "must pass on as a cheap present" books are stored. Rather frustratingly for me, since it's my job, evangelism for most Christians is simply not pleasant. For the vast majority of us it's either an activity that just isn't nice, or one that we struggle to know how to do, and then when we do it, it all seems like too much effort. I heard the founder of Street Pastors, Les Issacs describe evangelism like this: a "mission" that takes two years of hard graft in the planning and motivation for just two weeks of events and activity. The church then spends the following two years recovering from the two weeks' activities and a further two years planning for another "mission". Six years of planning for two weeks of gospel sharing! We were all in stitches at the absurdity of it all.

But, despite the unpopularity of the activity, there is no point in pretending that this book has any subject other than that of letting others know the love of God in Jesus Christ. I can't give this activity a name other than "evangelism". Believe me, if I could rename it, I would; quick as a flash. Of all the words used to describe something that every Christian is called to do, it has by far - and I mean by far - received the worst press and the most warped understanding of the lot. For many, the word is as popular as "flageliation" or "40 day fasts" or the "gift of celibacy". Even amongst those who don't profess the Christian faith the word is a bit of a no-no. For example, my wife and I went to our local summer's ball along with 400 other people. We sat at a table with ten people we didn't know and the charming lady I sat next to introduced herself and told me what she did for a living. She was fairly passionate about her counselling profession and after specifying all the 82 virtues of counselling, she said: "Don't worry; I'm not going to evangelise you about it!" She then asked what I did. It was a fairly awkward moment as I told her my profession. After an embarrassing pause, we both had a bit of a laugh about it. She had never met an evangelist before.

Calling the adventure of bringing life-giving words, works and wonders to people while working in partnership with the most beautiful, creative, powerful, accepting and healing man who has ever - and will ever - live "evangelism" is a bit like working for Rolls Royce crafting state-of-the-art car engines and calling it kit-car modelling. Since the word brings to mind so many negative images, some of my fellow evangelists have done away with that job title altogether and prefer to describe themselves, when asked, as "motivational speakers" or "lifestyle change coaches" or "marketing and advertising agents for Royalty"! (I made that last one up.) So, up front, I am an evangelist and I am not going to lull you into a false sense of security that this book is about anything other than evangelism, only in the closing chapters to reveal the true intention of the book and to take you on some kind of guilt trip to convince you to do evangelism because you really, really should. Rather, this book is about the adventure of serving a big-hearted God and showing his heart to others, not just through talking or making some kind of pitch at people, but rather through what we do together and how we work out together what it means to be a follower of Jesus.

My understanding of evangelism is that it is an activity which is rich, diverse, creative, fun, and involves partnership with the author of life himself. So, while I can't give evangelism another name, I certainly can give it another explanation. To do evangelism is to connect with others in a big-hearted way showing a big-hearted God. Yet so much of what has been labelled as evangelism is anything but that. Faith sharing in the past has been stingy, lazy, uncaring, and unkind. I don't just mean in projects run by churches, but as an action carried out by individuals who follow Christ. Often the way we engage with the world is unloving and holds people around us at arm's length. It seems as if the message that is good news has been delivered in a bad way. That's why many Christians of all shapes and sizes insist evangelism just isn't their cup of tea; they have seen it done badly, in small stingy-hearted ways, and this results in Christians being put off doing it and those who are not *in* just not getting what we are supposed to be trying to share with them.

Furthermore, small-hearted approaches to faith sharing aren't just found in the projects, talks and events we put on. People's ambivalence to the gospel and to what we have as Christians may also be down to how we communicate what it means to be Church. We need to be part of big-hearted churches. So many of us merrily carry on with structures and routines that are, on the whole, exclusively for the benefit of those who are in the know and so we exclude the majority of people in our communities. Take Sunday mornings, for example. Where-oh-where does the Bible decree that Sunday mornings are the set time for services to be held? Yet we hold on to the tradition that Sunday mornings are when Christians gather in a building, for a set routine of differing proportions - sing songs, pray, listen to a sermon - and then stay for a cup of tea and a biscuit at the end. So, what about the activity of going together to be church in our communities? What about being church for the sake of the community, engaging in activities that are outrageously for the benefit of those who are not *in* on what it means to be a Christian? What about changing the times we meet so that more people might gather with us? What about cancelling our set services and meeting in public places, accessible for people to ask questions and observe and take part?

By the way, have you ever thought about how daunting it must be for a person who has never been to your church to enter a church building?   It's familiar to you because you are part of it, but it may be very strange to someone else. I suggest you do one of the following, if you have never done so before, to help you empathise with the feelings of someone who is venturing on to your church turf for the first time.

1) Go and place a bet at a betting shop. 2) Get up early on Sunday morning and head down to your local car boot sale and see where the multitudes enjoy hanging out on a Sunday. 3) Visit a building of another faith, a Sikh temple or a mosque perhaps. Often, when I set challenges for people who are Christians to go and place a small bet in a betting shop, they come back quite upset. Some just didn't know what to do; others asked for help and didn't get any. Visiting another place of worship is fascinating. The only way I have coped is through asking questions about what is expected of me. At one mosque which I visited with friends we were placed on a stage for all to see as we went through the prayers and set routines - it was uncomfortable.

I believe we need a renewed desire for wanting to make sure that other people have what we have. To see more people gloriously and miraculously saved, as we have been, may require us to do church in a new way, a creative way and a big-hearted way, a way which is accessible and open to those of no faith. People are lost without Jesus and they need saving. How will they come to know God as their heavenly dad unless we start to do a new thing and engage with those in our communities in a way that is big-hearted? By the way, I keep meeting Christians who somehow have lost their conviction that people need saving. What's going on? They've reaped the benefits and enjoyed the gift, but somehow have come to believe that being saved isn't something that is on God's heart for the cosmos; it was just for them and a select few.

Maybe faith sharing is too scary for some; granted, it does mean venturing into the unknown, following Jesus to those who are bruised and battered by life, who need embracing and loving, and who need to hear some good news. Recently, I rearranged my diary so that, at least once a month on a Sunday, I venture into the city centre of Peterborough, with as many Christians as I can convince to join me, to engage with the vast majority of people who do not attend a church service. This means saying no to preaching invitations, and the opportunity to speak at events and conferences, so that I may meet first-time hearers of the gospel. This decision hasn't always been easy but I am convinced that this is an important part of what God is calling me to do.

Bit more of a preamble...

So, now you've had some preamble and the evangelism word is out in the open, here is even more preamble. It is worth noting at the beginning of this book what I actually mean by evangelism. Most definitions focus on the pitch, patter or presentation which suits events and church programmes, but I want to share a definition that is much broader than proclamation, although by stating this I'm not suggesting that the words we use to present the good news don't matter. This is the definition from my book, *Smack Heads and Fat Cats*:

> Evangelism is the overflow of devotion to Jesus that demonstrates him and his message to all people who do not know him so that they too may be disciples and decide to follow him, and like me, to be deployed to do his work.

Different facets of what evangelism entails and looks like are presented to you in this book in three sections. Now, I would love to write that this book had a most excellent plan right from the start, that it was crafted and shaped in the most considered way, intentionally shaped by two, oh so clever, people. Regrettably, that would be lying. Instead, this book has emerged from the journey of two guys who love Jesus, who desperately want to follow him more and more, and who want others to join us in this adventure too.

To be honest, and to use this page as a bit of a therapeutic disclaimer and confession, if I had to describe how this book has been formed it would be: a pouring out. It is a gushing out of all that has been bubbling away, a presenting in word form of gut-feelings and hunches about what we believe God is saying to his Church. So, this is a prophetic pouring out rather than an academic thesis; it is more akin to a heartfelt plea to our brothers and sisters to let others who don't yet follow Jesus in on what we have, than a clever theory to convince you.

Therefore, with the confession out of the way, you may wonder whether this book is really necessary. Well, I believe it is. We live in desperate times where some people in this world serve and know a big-hearted loving God, whom they call Father, while the majority of people just haven't got a clue about him. While they may have heard something about him and may have some kind of inkling that there must be something out there or have had experiences of God's goodness in their lives, the Christian faith still remains a mystery.

It's just not right that the majority of people have yet to hear and see the good news of Jesus. We must make sense of their searchings and longings and introduce them to the God who became a person to be amongst us, who wants them, and longs for them to know him as the best dad they could ever have imagined or hoped for. If this book gives you the impetus to let others enjoy what you have as a Christian than I am chuffed as can be.

Over the last 18 months or so, my co-author, Simon, and I have met on and off to seek God, to talk and to imagine what a book about being big-hearted would look like. So, we came up with an outline. Afterwards while enjoying a cup of tea, I shared with Simon that somehow it would be great if the book could follow the simple pattern of the "up, in and out" life-shape so wonderfully developed by Mike Breen and others at St Thomas' in Sheffield. Not that I wanted to copy their writings, but rather to develop the theme of healthy Christian living where evangelism was an integral part of our lives. When I suggested this, Simon gave me a puzzled look and then gently (and slowly) explained that our plan was very much following these three principles of a life lived with devotion to God, building community with one another, and looking out to those who don't have a clue about what it means to be a follower of Christ. I tried to cover up my lack of understanding and made a joke about how unobservant I am when it comes to my own planning; but it was awkward. So rather by chance, this book is written in three parts:

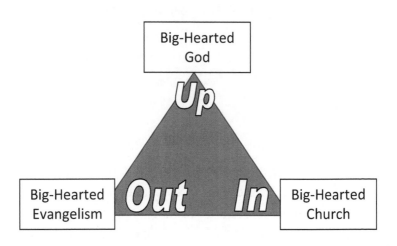

1. What does it mean to serve a Big-hearted God? This section chooses three characteristics of what God is like: God is love, he is our Father, and he is good.

2. What does a Big-hearted church look like? Simon Goddard bases this section upon the five core values that came out of a consultation within the Baptist Union of Great Britain back in 1996 and re-examines these values from a big-hearted perspective. He identifies that to be a big-hearted church we need to be a community that is: 1) gospel telling; 2) gospel dwelling; 3) generously giving; 4) grace growing; and 5) glory glowing.

3. The final section of this book is based on Big-hearted evangelism. It spells out four convictions about evangelism:

1) it sees God in others.

2) it seeks to do the works of Jesus.

3) it is a participatory activity.

4) it is about being integral with who we are.

Lastly, it's worth saying that throughout the book we have wanted to show some examples of what we are writing about, ideas to copy and have a go at, and some stories of people who epitomise what it means to be big-hearted followers of Jesus.

BIG
HEARTED

SECTION 1

Big-Hearted God

Why Big-Hearted God?

This is how God showed his love among us: He sent his one and only Son into the world that we might live through him. This is love: not that we loved God, but that he loved us and sent his Son as an atoning sacrifice for our sins.

1 John 4:9 & 10

My first guest at the café church in my local town joined us by accident. Jane was hung-over, bored and just needed to kill some time. However, the side effects of her alcohol-fuelled late night didn't dampen my enthusiasm in the slightest and my small team decided to press on with our "gathering" with zeal, albeit with an amended programme. First of all we ditched the team quiz as, with just one guest, the competition would be rubbish. However, I didn't throw out the theme and stuck with: how to have peace.

After talking together for half an hour and sharing stories, we had lost track somewhat and it was than a thought came into my head: I could ask this lady a question that would be brilliantly clever, cause the conversation to deepen, and bring us back to the theme of peace. "Jane, if there was one question that you could ask God, what would it be?" Boom, I thought, that's captured the conversation! What a good reasonable question to ask; clever me. However, the pause was long and awkward as Jane sat there, sipped on her coffee and pondered my query. Eventually she answered by asking me a question. She said, quite exasperated: "Well, IF there is a God, what is IT like?" Her question was like a sharp slap around the chops of my heart. I had asked a question thinking Jane had some kind of idea that there could be a God and that she might have some inkling of what he is like, but her response was a million and one miles away from my perception. After talking some more, her response didn't seem odd; she explained that she didn't have any Christian friends and no one in her family had ever been to church before.

Jane's question is an important one to grapple with. "What is IT like?" How would you answer the question? You see, as followers of Jesus we need to have some idea and confidence about what God is like. How we live out being a Christian is governed by what we believe; in other words, our theology informs how we live and the message we have to share with those around us. Gerard Hughes in 'God of Surprises' writes that as Christians we need to pray that we may rid ourselves of false notions of God. He argues that this isn't just an intellectual process, but one where our whole beings are affected: it shapes the way we view ourselves, other people and the world. Hughes caricatures three typical ideas Christians can have about God. One (which he made as an identikit while listening to Catholic students at a university) is a fearful uncle whom he calls George. George insists that he is visited once a week in his old cold mansion and demands devotion, or else there will be punishment. Secondly, God may seem like Santa Claus, a kindly figure who enters life occasionally to give us presents. The third is a policeman type God, whose predominant interest is in our faults.

Let me highlight a caricature of my own, based on an idea which is held by Christians I have met. It's a skewed notion that God dislikes those who are not spiritually clean and, at best, keeps *sinners* at arm's length, if he lets them anywhere near him at all. This is a selective God, one who has favourites, but dislikes most people. Holding this belief would affect the way we engage with our workmates every day. When I first became a Christian I somehow developed some of this thinking about people who were not Christians, when I read in the Bible about "heathens having worthless thoughts". (I may have imagined this passage or made it up, as now I can't find it anywhere in the Bible!) Needless to say, this really didn't make me the life and soul of the party at all, and I remember having a "you wouldn't understand" kind of attitude to anyone who wasn't a Christian - awful. I even remember writing in the condensation of a bus shelter window some unfriendly quotes from the Bible for my unsaved barbarian friends to admire. You could say I had some kind of condemnation-in-condensation ministry.

My new-found zeal as a Christian led me to be rather unloving for a short time, which I admit is a strange attitude to have, but that was in the past. In the present, I am puzzled by some of the insights we have accepted as truth about God and his thoughts towards humankind. For example, suppose you have a perception that God doesn't particularly like the gay, lesbian and bi-sexual people in your community. How would this affect your engagement with them? Suppose you thought that God didn't approve of healing people unless they were *right* with him or that they needed to be part of the church first. How would this affect your prayers for those around you? What if you thought that people who were living together were *living in sin* and couldn't come to know God until their lives were sorted out and they slept in separate beds? What chances would these groups of people have of encountering the good news of Jesus from you before they encountered a challenge about their lifestyle and behaviour? Or suppose you thought that people with tattoos and piercings couldn't come to know God and had somehow cursed themselves through breaking the law set out in Leviticus 19:28, which states: "Do not cut your bodies for the dead or put tattoo marks on yourself, I am the LORD." How would this affect your attitude towards those around you? Would they hear the gospel from your lips?

You see, all these examples, just like people you may know in your community, regardless of their sexuality, lifestyle, behaviour or appearance, are loved by God. God is in very nature love. Too often as followers of Jesus we exclude people from hearing about our faith and therefore from having the chance to become Christians, because our perception is that they are somehow beyond the pale and cannot be *in*. We conclude that their lifestyles exclude them; full stop. That's it: they're *out*, despite not knowing there's an alternative. But that's simply not right. If we hold on to false perceptions of who can be *in* and who is *out*, then we make God out to be stingy and only for those who behave correctly. We need to get back to what the Bible teaches us: that all people are able to come to know God as their Father through Jesus Christ. It's just that most people don't know that. Jesus challenged this perception of who could know God and who couldn't when he declared: "It is not the healthy who need a doctor, but the sick. I have not come to call the righteous, but sinners." (Mark 2:17) His declaration jarred on the ears of those who were grumbling and moaning about the company he kept and the kind of people he was willing to eat with and dedicate his time to. If you think that is ridiculous, bring the situation up to date. Imagine what reaction you would receive from people in your church if next week you had lunch with some of the ladies or pimps from the red-light district of your nearest city. You see, Jesus redefined holiness – changing it from a separate state away from all things unclean, to a place where love and acceptance are found in the filthiest of places. If Jesus is holy (and he is), then obviously holiness is not about separation, but rather about the opposite. The sort of company Jesus kept earned him a bad reputation: "The Son of Man came, eating and drinking, and people say, 'Look at him! He eats too much and drinks too much wine, and he is a friend of tax collectors and sinners.' But wisdom is proved to be right by what she does." (Matthew 11:19 CEV)

Such then is the nature of a holy God who is love, revealed through his son, Jesus. He pours out his grace upon the least deserving people - like me and you. Every person who has ever lived, and who ever will live, is way beyond any hope of spending eternity in heaven, as people are born into sinfulness which separates them from holy God. That's a universal condition. Yet the heart of the gospel of undeserved love, I believe, needs pouring into our hearts yet again. The majority of people in the world don't know that they can come to know God because they haven't been included, told or discipled in the Christian faith. People need Jesus; yet many of us we carry on our day-to-day lives as if people are better off without him.

The Bible is chock-a-block full of stories about those who have been saved and yet are people with whom you would least expect to be rubbing shoulders on a Sunday morning. The very first non-Jewish Christian was an Ethiopian eunuch. Shocking! Having been castrated as a boy, he would have grown up looking more like a woman than a man, with wider hips and larger breasts. His job was to look after the beds of the harem, where people would have multiple sexual partners. Yet, he wasn't excluded from heaven by Philip's big-hearted approach to sharing faith and then baptising him too.

What about Paul? Without the gift of grace, the author of much of the New Testament would have remained a self-righteous religious murderer. What about Peter? He was a hot tempered zealot who under pressure denied Jesus and cursed his name. What about the prostitute who anointed Jesus' feet with a very expensive jar of perfume? She's so famous that Jesus declared that wherever the gospel is preached throughout the world what she did will also be told in memory of her. (Matthew 26:13) The gospel changed people then, and still does today. Let me explain, through a story, how our perception of who God is can affect how we engage with people.

Greg asked me to tattoo a cross on him. He is one of the biggest hearted people I have met recently, a gentle Buddhist who owns a tattoo and piercing parlour. He and his fellow artists have welcomed me, as the city centre chaplain of Peterborough, into their shop so generously and lovingly. The kettle is always on for me and even when people are madly busy I am still welcomed to chill for a bit on their amazingly comfy sofa.

So, here I am in his shop, in shock, trying to consider Greg's request. It just seems so weird because of my total lack of tattoo experience. Yet, despite my feeble attempts to explain that I really don't know what to do or whether I could actually do something like a tattoo, he insists that I am just

the man to do the job. Greg explains that he wants a
of hope. He says that, since every time I visit his shop
hope and "great vibes", he wants a permanent reminder
At that moment, right in the midst of the busy tattoo sh
tears fill my eyes. "I'm so humbled," I say, and then, while
wondering whether a Baptist minister is allowed to tattoo
someone, I agree to it. You see, God loves Greg and wants to
be his Father.

As I knelt down ready to tattoo him, I held Greg's foot with
one of my hands and the inked tattoo gun in the other. As my
hands shook as I prepared to draw a permanent cross on him,
he poured out his heart and explained some of the hurt he
had gone through. The tattoo was a mess, yet it didn't seem to
matter because I had felt the unmistakable presence of the
King who washed feet. Despite the fact that Greg was in pain
through my cack-handed attempt at tattooing and had blood
pouring from his ankle, I felt the Holy Spirit right next to me.

Afterwards Jay, who had been next to me and who had
guided and helped me to tattoo Greg, said: "Now, you can tick
that off your list of things to do." I replied: "It wasn't even on
my list." This surprise encounter made me realise that I need
to be willing to go into new places and to do new things for
the sake of the people who need an opportunity to *get* this
wonderful good-news story that requires a response. Even
though some of the lines of the crudely drawn cross didn't
meet, Greg thanked me for the tattoo and since then has
proudly shown me and others the clumsily tattooed cross.

when I bumped into him in the city, he

'n front of his friends: "This is the priest

g of God affects our witness and our

‸ around us which is why this first section is

‸ ιo looking at big-hearted God. I believe God is love. ∩e is Father. He is good. I have only chosen three characteristics of God. I know there are many, many more. There is so much of God which is a mystery that we haven't fathomed because God is, well, God. We can never grow tired of working out what God is like; our experience and understanding of him never reaches a place where we say: "Yep, I've got it! I don't need to know anything else about God as I've worked him all out." My choice of these three out of all his characteristics is deliberate and, I believe, vital for us as we engage with people in our post-Christian culture. It is imperative that the news of the God of love, who gave his Son for this world to rescue us and reconcile us to himself, doesn't remain a secret. People just do not know or connect with the idea that there could be a God who loves them, who aches to be their Father and who is good. This news is certainly new to the majority of people around us. I believe that this state of ignorance in our cities, towns and villages should compel us to do something. It's simply not right that people don't know. The simplicity of living out, with confidence, these characteristics of God, personally, as well as in our relationships and gatherings will, I believe, let others see what we believe and let them catch a glimpse of what it means to be someone who *believes in God*. In other words, if people are to *get* what we have, then we need to emphasise these core characteristics of God for the sake of a world that is lost and so much in need.

In my own journey as a Christian I seek to know more of the love of God. Last year I went on one of my monthly prayer walks for the day. I was burdened and needed to ask God a question. "Why is all this good stuff happening to me? Why do I have so many opportunities to preach and teach? Why have I had opportunities to talk on radio, to write and share my convictions about evangelism with more and more people? Why, God?" I stood still and waited for an answer, hoping that God would somehow speak to me. I stood for a while and closed my eyes on a deserted path by a field. It was cold, yet bright and the wind was whistling round me. Then I heard him ... softly ... whispering into my very being, yet thunderously loud, filling all of me. "Because..." I held my breath. "Because... you love me and I love you." All the burdens, all the stressed-out thoughts that somehow all the favour in what was happening was down to something I'd done, all the weight of responsibility, just rolled off. It was a good feeling: the simplicity of my love for my heavenly Father and his love for me. This experience and knowledge of love affects how I am.

Reg, the Sainsbury's delivery man had time to stay and have a cup of tea. He asked what I was up to, so I told him that I was writing a book about being big-hearted. He shared with me how he didn't understand people who followed a God of whom they lived in fear and didn't enjoy. He spoke about some friends who were "religious", yet lived by rules and regulations and were worried that God was going to get them and be upset with them when they broke the rules. I shared about the three characteristics of God that I believe are important, that he is love, is good and is like a dad. Reg said: "Now that's what I believe that God is like." Then there was a long pause, before he said: "If I did believe in God that is."

God is love

God is love. Jesus came because of God's love. We go where God sends us because of God's love. It is as simple as that. God's love is the key message, and all we have to do is help people respond to it.[1] (Jim Currin)

I finished my street performance in the middle of Norwich on a hot summer's day and jumped around exuberantly, slightly hot and sweaty, holding above my head the straight-jacket from which I had just escaped. It was a good show and I looked around awaiting the cheers, but on this occasion the small crowd gave polite applause more suited to a cricket match then a wild escape challenge with blaring music from Florence and The Machine. Until two ladies with a dog staggered by who shouted and cheered their hearts out and then came and sat down right in front of me. They looked somewhat wasted. I wondered what to do; then I thought the best thing would be to ask them what they thought about my show. "What show?" said one lady. Great, they hadn't seen any of it. They asked what I had been doing, so I quickly shared about my hope to show something of my faith and what Jesus had done in my life. I spoke about how much God loved people. "God!" cried one lady. "There is no ******* God! How can you say that there is a God? You don't know he exists!" she snarled. We sat down together on the steps, me in my clown's costume and these two ladies with their dog.

"Why don't we ask God to be with us?" I asked. As soon as I said that one of the ladies looked at the other and said: "Hang on, what's going on here? I feel … sober." It turned out that they had both been drinking and popping pills all morning and now sat with me, the clown, experiencing clear heads. One lady quickly suggested that we pray, and hold hands to ask God to meet with us. As we held hands, one lady asked: "Can you pray in that strange language, tongues?" I said that I did and they asked if I would pray over them. Then they both bowed their heads and closed their eyes, still holding my hands; waiting. I sang a song in tongues over them and as soon as I had done that one lady looked at me and I asked what was happening. "I feel so loved," she declared. The other lady just smiled and sat still, and then, after a while, she described the most beautiful sensation all over her. It was as if I had just witnessed a loving father scoop up his girls and hold them close. As I basked in the presence of God with these two ladies, still holding their hands, I noticed a fight break out near an art piece I was doing on the streets. So I got up and quickly introduced them to a lady who was working on the team and who came from one of the local churches. The next day I was back on the streets and I heard that the two ladies had asked Jesus into their lives and had continued experiencing his love in the most tangible way. The lady who had prayed with them spoke with me, and said, assuming I had known all along: "It was so good you prayed with those two prostitutes."

I wonder how two prostitutes who were drunk would have been dealt with by God before the gift of love in Jesus came to this world? If caught with a married man, the law would have found them guilty and they would have been put to death by stoning. Yet, before my very eyes, the same God who once decreed a harsh punishment, made sure that they were beautifully rescued by him and basked in his great love for them. When the early Christians were working out who and what God was and how they could relate to him, there was a writer called Marcion who added some thoughts to the debate. He concluded that Christianity was a religion of love, and that love had no place in the legalistic law of the Old Testament. He decided that there must be two Gods. One who was the God of the Hebrew scripture, and the other the Christian God revealed in Jesus, whose job it was to depose the God of the law and to usher in the worship of the true God of grace. Marcion was quickly excommunicated as a heretic and the teaching of the one true God who has always been, always is, and always will be, was restored. He asked the right question, but got the wrong answer. A quick overview of some of the stories of God in the Old Testament finds God commanding ethnic cleansing, imposing wars and the killing of woman and children, and ordering the complete annihilation of entire cities. Even when people accidentally touched the place where he dwelt, they died.

Compare this with God revealed through Jesus Christ where you have a God who teaches love for our enemies, turning the other cheek, blessing those who curse us, and laying down our lives for the sake of others. Jesus is the God of love whom people reached out to touch and everyone who did found healing and wholeness.

Yet, the God of the Old and the New Testament is the same one. So how do we reconcile God's different characteristics and temperament? I believe this dichotomy is reconciled in a single act in history, the carrying out of the most amazing rescue plan this world has ever, or will ever, experience - when Jesus laid down his life and died upon a cross. It is only in the light of the new covenant in the blood of Jesus that the love of God is fully revealed in the Old Testament. Reading it without the knowledge of the new covenant might leave you thinking God is hateful. Yet, the Hebrew scriptures show that, because of love, God set in place a law that could never be fulfilled, so that one day he would bring the world close to his heart through his Son. Only through Jesus can the entire law be fulfilled. The God of love always knew that there was a rescue plan to redeem and make all things new, a plan by which an imperfect people could find their way home, justified and made perfect through a holy sinless Son, to a holy all powerful Father. The cross of Christ reveals, in time,

God's eternal character and purpose He utterly gives himself for the world's good and salvation.

All the struggles and hardship associated with God fashioning a people out of the nations of the world, all the harshness and God's desire for obedience from his people, all the punishment when people got it wrong or turned away from him, all of this had a purpose. God carefully crafted a chosen people for himself because they would one day be given a Messiah. This saviour in turn would be a gift to the whole world, not just to Israel, and all people would be able to know about salvation and the way back to a holy, loving perfect God; relationship restored. Furthermore, God didn't stand aloof in this process. He himself was poured out for us. Get this: a holy, all powerful, creator God humbled himself and become a man to live among us and to rescue us. That is truly *kenotic* (self-emptying), an expression of the most lavish love.

Perhaps you have a problem being confident that, since God's character is perfect, he can love all people. I must admit that I struggle with the idea that all people are loved. I met a witch who happily divulged some of the activities she was involved in and how good she thought the devil was. Could this person be even liked by God, I wondered. I met her when I was with a small team on the streets handing out pots of earth where people could plant sunflowers, a small gift that would grow over the months and remind people that the good news of Jesus grows and grows like a seed. A cheerful sign declared: "Come and plant a sunflower!" To add to the experience a friend of mine wrote words of knowledge for people on the pots, but then placed them in a large tub to give them out randomly to those who joined us in a seed-sowing. I questioned her about this, and asked whether she could write them on each one as we met people, rather than giving them out randomly. "God knows which pot is for which person," she declared confidently. So, as she reached for a pot of earth to give to the witch and her boyfriend, I imagined what the message would declare. "Turn from your sins," I thought, or "The devil is defeated!" As she clasped the pot of earth, I tried to make out what was written on it. "What does it say?" I enquired innocently; sure it would be an appropriate rebuke. "I don't understand what it means," the witch said, and handed me the pot. Aha, my chance to admonish her sinful ways, I thought, as I looked down - and on the pot I read "grace".

For a while we spoke with this lady about the undeserved gift of God, given for all through Jesus; a free gift of grace because we are so loved. She was amazed by the message. You too may struggle to think all people can be loved by God. I'm not sure what you thought when you read at the beginning of the story: "I met a witch." Don't get me wrong, I believe that, when we die, we will be held accountable for all our actions and for what each one of us has done with the gift of grace, but for now God longs for all his children to be made right with him.

The behaviour and sinfulness of people around us and what they are involved in may cause us to question whether they are loved by God; portions of scripture from the Old Testament may also make us question whether all people are equal in the sight of a loving Father. If this is something we struggle with then it is important to know that the scriptures revealed in the Old can never take authority over the teachings of the New. The New Covenant revealed in Jesus Christ is the last word. Glen Marshall writes that not everything we read in the Bible is equally important. "That kind of flatlander approach to Christianity ends up with such silliness as inerrancy and, if we are not careful, a crushing legalism. It really couldn't be much plainer: what matters most is loving God with everything we've got, loving other people the same way and making the purposes of God our top priority. Other stuff matters, of course it does, but not as much as this. Jesus said."[2]

Jesus is the ultimate revelation of what God is like, so as followers of him, if we want to get to grips with what God is in to and what he desires of us, then we need to get to grips with Jesus. Why? He shows us the Father. The beginnings of the books of John, Colossians, Hebrews and Revelation highlight this principle:

- Jesus was with God in the beginning, is God and everything has been made through him and he is life, the light to all people (John 1:1-3)

- Jesus is the image of the invisible God, the first born over all creation, God had all his fullness dwell in him (Colossians 1:15)

- Jesus is the radiance of God's glory, the exact representation of God's being (Hebrews 1:3)

- Jesus is the Alpha and Omega. John writes that on seeing the risen Jesus he fell at his feet as though dead, while Jesus declares, "I am the First and the Last. I am the Living One; I was dead, and behold I am alive for ever and ever!" (Revelation 1:18)

Philip struggled with the idea that the man he had spent the last three years with was actually God. The conversation recorded in John 14 always makes me smile. Jesus is telling his first friends that he is the way, truth and life, that anyone who wants to come to the Father has to come through him. Philip then asks for directions. I swear, if they had had buses in those times, he would have asked for a timetable and where the bus stop was. "Show us the Father, and that will be enough for us." (John 14:8) Jesus' response is just amazing: "You've been with me this long and you make such a stupid request! Don't you know me or what!" (my translation) and then Jesus declares: "Anyone who has seen me has seen the Father." (John 14:9)

So if we are to believe in a big-hearted God who is love, then we need to look to Jesus for the practical outworking of what that love looks like. What can Jesus reveal to us about God's love?

Firstly, human life is of great value. Jesus considers people he meets in the most high, extraordinarily lavish way. We take it for granted that Jesus just couldn't help but love people perfectly. No one was turned away. Imagine if we read in Luke 5 that Jesus told the man who begged for healing with the words, "...if you are willing, you can make me clean," to "BOG OFF!" "Nope, I'm not willing, it's tough, you're just going to have to live with it, loser ..." We would be shocked. It's just that Jesus always *was* willing. The actual response, by the way, quotes Jesus as saying: "I am willing... be clean!" Immediately the leprosy leaves the man who called out to him. We have just got used to Jesus' kindness. He loves people and accepts them. When the disciples thought that children shouldn't bother him, he made it clear that the kingdom was exactly for them. The irony of this is that the very disciples who tried to exclude the hugging, jumping kids were not who you would expect to be hanging out with the King of the Cosmos. They were a mixture of uneducated fishermen and tax collectors being taught by the Saviour of the world. I love it.

How can we show something of the extent of the love of God in what we do? One of the ways I engage with people is to show their worth. Take, for example, the red carpet with a big "VIPs Only" sign that I have set up in a city centre. People gather around waiting to see who the very important people are that are going to turn up. They are surprised when they hear it is them. "Why am I important?" most people ask.

Another favourite activity of mine that I love to do to show people's worth is to set up a sign that says: "I will listen." Here's the story of the first time I did it:

9am Sunday morning and I'm literally wrestling with a sofa, trying to get it on top of the car. It's so stubborn and heavy and I'm hot and bothered. To top it all, my wife, who is rather grudgingly helping me and also trying to lift the heavy beast of a sofa, isn't too pleased with the whole sofa idea. With a sweaty brow, I begin to question whether my idea of taking it into the centre of Peterborough is really such a bright one. However, with the sofa finally loaded and tied on to the top of my car, I set off with the hope that: 1) the sofa doesn't fall off and cause some kind of horrific traffic jam; and 2) I will be able to meet people throughout the morning and early afternoon to share something of my faith.

10.30am - the sofa is on the street and covered with a white sheet and an England flag to hide the fact that it's an old battered pink tatty thing that I picked up off free-cycle and has cigarette burn marks and some worryingly odd and dubious stains. However, it looks like new with a bright white cover and I'm quite chuffed with the spectacle it makes. I am joined by a deacon from the local Baptist Church, who is also a youth worker in the city. With some shoppers giving us some curious looks and some giving us happy smiles we sit on the sofa and pray for the day.

11.30am - an hour in, the response has been positive. Not a great deal of listening, but lots of intrigue!

1.00pm - We are inundated with people! Groups of young people take it in turn to sit on the sofa and talk; two ladies ask for their picture to be taken on it and then stay for 45 minutes to talk and talk. They have so many questions and are confused about what to believe in life. True to my word, I listen. When they ask, I talk about Jesus. They talk some more and I listen. In the end, they agree that we should pray together and in the middle of a city centre, on a settee, we pray for God to draw close to us and I pray that he would show how much he loves them. When they leave they are happy and they take a copy of Mark's gospel with them too.

2.00pm - Two groups of young people have hung out with us for some time now. It feels as though we have made friends as we talk about life and what's been happening. One young lad has been kicked out of his home and we point him to support services for housing. We swap Facebook details and arrange to meet up again soon.

2.30pm - Time to pack up. We have a final sit on the sofa and give thanks for the people we have met and the conversations we have had. Then, once more, I wrestle the sofa onto the car and head off home.

Secondly, Jesus shows that the practical outworking of believing that God is a God of love means that people are not excluded. People were welcome to join Jesus wherever he went. The only constraints seemed to be whether the building was full, and even then, once, a roof was vandalised and some men lowered a friend of theirs in front of Jesus for him to heal. I've been thinking about the story where Jesus is teaching 5,000 people all day long, and then decides they need feeding because they're hungry. There just doesn't seem to be a guest list or a perimeter around the mountain with the larger disciples acting as bouncers at the gate to make sure that those who are not on the list don't come in. It's a daft thought I know, but it just seems so contrary to how we do what we do. People are excluded from many of our meetings and gatherings, not on purpose, but because we hide away behind closed doors. Yet, there was absolutely no exclusion on the mountainside. Were people declined when they came to share in the bread and fish because of their lifestyle or what they happened to believe about God or not? The Bible states that "they all ate and were satisfied." (Luke 9:17)

Because I spent a good portion of the first seven or so years of my ministry on the streets with young people and people who were homeless, I ended up being involved in the most heart-breaking of circumstances. Once I was asked to lead some kind of remembrance for two lads who used to come occasionally to our drop in lunch. They had died in the toilets by the bus station after they had taken some heroin that was cut with poison and other junk. I arranged a gathering in the local park by a tree; around 30 people turned up. We stood in a big circle; I said a few words and gave everyone a white flower to place by a tree in memory of them. I also had two pure white balloons and invited people to come up and hold the string of the balloons and say goodbye; most did. I had planned to pronounce a blessing over the gathered crowd, but, before I could, a large spliff was lit as some kind of temporary memorial for the two young lads and passed round the circle for all to take a puff. Then a can of Special Brew lager was opened and poured out as some kind of offering, in remembrance. It was deeply moving and these two emblems, while destructive in themselves, carried, for that moment, some kind of holy significance and strangely complimented the white flowers and balloons. After this, I pronounced the blessing over my congregation and told them how valuable and important their lives were; that they truly mattered.

Should I have asked for the impromptu symbols of the spliff and the lager to have been put away?

Thirdly, the love of God revealed in Jesus seems to show preferential treatment to those on the margins. It's not that people who are well and rich are excluded; it's rather that the emphasis that Jesus placed in what he said and the way he embraced those who would have been considered as outcasts, seem to suggest that to believe in a God of love is to reach out to those who are poor and marginalised. The scriptures reveal something of God's heart for exiles, widows, orphans and the sick.[3] Wallis argues that our faithfulness to Scripture is, "...finally tested not by dogma and doctrine but by how one's life demonstrates that he or she believes the Bible. Belief results in obedience. In wealthy nations, that fidelity will best be tested by our relationship to the poor."[4]

If we believe in a God of love, our behaviour towards others will need to match. We certainly need more and more of this characteristic in our lives. In his book, *The Revolution of Love*, George Verwer argues that this message of love is the basic ingredient which is largely lacking in Christianity today and that this is the source of most of our problems. I couldn't agree more. Even in my short time of being a Baptist minister, I have seen too many Christians talk of God's love, sing heartily of how amazing it is, and yet fail to show it through their engagement with fellow human beings around them. We can believe something all we want; it is only made real when we live it out.

There's an old myth that John the apostle was much in demand and was often asked to speak to the emerging groups of believers. His diary was booked solid and he had to prioritise where he would speak. But after a few years he started to have more and more free time and wasn't asked to visit church groups as much, and soon the invitations dried up all together. You see, his sermons were always the same. "Not again," people would whisper under their breath, as John introduced his teaching by saying: "I'm going to talk to you today about love!" In his gospel, John records Jesus as saying: "My command is this: love each other as I have loved you." (John 15:12) "A new command I give you: Love one another. As I have loved you, so you must love one another. By this all men will know that you are my disciples, if you love one another." (John 13:34,35) In his letters, this message is emphasised over and over again.

His first letter: "This is the message you heard from the beginning: We should love one another." 1 John 3:11

His second letter: "... I am not writing to you a new command, but one that we have had from the beginning. I ask that we love one another." 2 John v5

His third letter: He commends the church about what they believe, as some visitors "... have told the church about your love". 3 John v6

John's reiteration of the theme of love is one that is apt for today. You see, he wasn't wasting valuable Bible space when he wrote: "Dear friends, I am not writing you a new command but an old one, which you have had from the beginning." (1 John 2:7) This old command was repeated over and over because the Christians back then kept forgetting and presumably kept doing the opposite. We need to grasp this distinguishing trait of what God is like and then live it out, to prove our belief in the way that we see ourselves and others, as loved by God. We need the God of love to soak our very beings so that others can see what he is like through us. Jim Currin emphasises this need for what we believe about being loved to then, in turn, affect our faith sharing: "When we are sharing our faith, both our words and our actions should be characterised by love. Love is the first element of the good news, it is key to people listening, receiving and understanding the truth of the gospel."[5]

God is good

For the LORD is good and his love endures forever; his faithfulness continues through all generations.
Psalm 100:5

On a few occasions last year I presented to members of the public what they can get from God. I make a free fruit stall: hundreds of pieces of nine kinds of fruit in boxes set out like a market stall. It looks vibrant and the big "Free Fruit" sign attracts many people. On approaching the stall most people are fascinated by what they see, as each fruit is labelled with one of the following: "love, joy, peace, patience, kindness, goodness, faithfulness, gentleness, self-control". (Galatians 5:22-23) Some people merrily help themselves to armfuls of fruit and thank us for the free gift; others ponder and read through the labels, and then ask why the fruit is labelled with all those good things. I gently explain that this is what we can have from God. One lady stood looking at the stall for a few minutes and then asked, "Could I please have that apple?" I said that she could just help herself. "Great," she said with a sigh of relief, "I really need peace."

The fact that God is good is for most people a secret. I want to shout it out: God is good! We need to be sure of this fact in our desire to be big-hearted. If we engage with people about our faith and the message of the good news while believing that God isn't quite up to scratch then our message will be skew-whiff. Do we really believe in a good God? Or do we believe that God punishes, hurts and condemns people? It's become something of an institutionalised chant in many non-institutional churches that if you mention "God is good", even over a cup of coffee at the end of a service, then someone somewhere will shout out "all the time". The standard unwritten liturgical response is then: "All the time ..." and then they in turn get to announce: "God is good!" It's cheesy and can be slightly annoying; the important thing is - it's true!

I recently led a small team on the streets on a Sunday morning offering messages of hope. We had written on over 100 stones some simple words of hope that we prayed would connect with people and help them. We stacked these stones on a plinth and invited people who were out and about doing their shopping to help themselves to one; it was simple. One lady with a little girl came up to the stack of stones and considered the signs declaring that under each one was a message of hope. She randomly reached out for one and read it. She then stood still and seemed to be in shock, mouth wide open. Some of the team asked if anything was the matter and she showed her stone to them. "Keep going" were the words on the bottom. She began to weep as she explained that she had breast cancer and had been despairing, feeling as if God were punishing her. You see, her idea of God was of a god who was angry and upset by any mistakes she made, and so the cancer she had was a way of her being punished severely. The team members gently reassured her that God wasn't like that, but rather he loved her and wanted her to be made well again. They prayed with her and that short encounter left her feeling reassured that God was with her and wanted to help her in the pain and trauma of cancer.

I have trained many Christians in evangelism over the years and often encourage them to consider their own journey to faith. I guarantee that 99% came to faith because they believed at some point that God was good and deeply interested in their lives. People come to a realisation that somehow he knows them inside and out and *still* loves them to bits. We don't become Christians thinking that the main focus of our devotion is a God who is bad, unkind and ready to punish us for the slightest mistake.

Laurence Singlehurst in his popular book of the 90s, *Sowing, Reaping, Keeping*, taught that in our evangelism the first goal to help others on their spiritual journey is to show G.I.G and C.A.O.K. - God Is Good and Christians Are OK! Emphasis on this characteristic of God is vital as many hold a perception of God that is untrue, seeing him as bad, vengeful, unhappy and ready to beat people with a big stick if they do anything too naughty. The second part of this first goal is to show that Christians are okay and not just a bunch of nutjobs who are into some fantasy fairy world. This can take some doing!

While this first step in doing evangelism may seem too over-simplistic, I have taken it on board in most of the things I do. Surprisingly, I meet people who are willing to engage with something of the gospel and, in doing so, have their perceptions changed about what it means to be a Christian.

By the way, the number one question I am asked by other Christians when they find out I'm a street evangelist is: "What response do you get on the streets? Are people unkind or angry towards you?" Since most of what I do is simply loving people and showing the goodness of God, I can honestly say the response is amazingly positive. Some people who wouldn't describe themselves as Christians have, on a few occasions, made a point of saying to me something like: "Thank you for showing your faith in this way on the streets." Why do I do it? Because I long to show others the goodness of God!

Take a few minutes to consider this challenge: do you know for yourself that God is good? It may seem like an odd question to ask, yet I meet people who have been Christians for most of their lives and they still believe that God really doesn't like them very much. They are unsure whether they are loved and whether God is good and this affects how they relate to those around them who are not Christians. Yet, why does this matter? Am I nit-picking in some overly psychological way over what individual Christians believe?

Let me explain my passion in this matter: knowing God as good means that as Christians we are prepared to receive his goodness into our lives and then pass it on. We serve a big-hearted God who desires that his goodness is known throughout the world. It's down to us to share that goodness. Furthermore, knowing about this goodness means when we encounter situations that are not, we have a means of measuring what's right and what's not.

For example, take my friend Jim. Recently he and I stood in the street and listened to a long story of heartache from a man who had lived on the streets, but was now in need of a bed for his new flat. However, whatever he tried to do to get the various furnishings he needed, it just didn't work out. It seemed very complicated to arrange delivery and no one could help him move things into his first floor flat. Having listened, my friend Jim boldly declared: "God doesn't want you to be miserable. He wants you to have a safe home, with all the things you need." I was struck by his confidence. Jim then proceeded to work out with the man a way to sort out the problems he was encountering. Jim then asked if he could pray for the man. I was quite surprised when the man said yes; he seemed very willing to have some prayer. I must admit that I thought Jim's very positive take on sorting out the accommodation mess was somewhat over the top. Until I heard Jim's prayer, which was a celebration of God's goodness and a statement of what God wanted for this man's life. It was powerful to watch and I learnt something that day.

If God is good, then this should be the measure for how we engage with difficulties and suffering.

Yet, how does this simple theology help us to know what to do with the bad stuff that still happens to all kinds of people? I have found that hope in God's goodness helps me hold on even in the roughest of times. Last year, after I had preached at a service, I had the honour of being asked to pray for a couple from South Africa. As soon as I started to pray tears rolled down the weathered kind face of the husband. His wife held his hand lovingly and nodded as I spoke some words that I believed were on God's heart for them. I felt that this man would become like a father to many men who had never had one, that people who hadn't been told of their worth or hadn't been embraced by the kind strong arms of a loving dad would be brought to him. In short, I saw him as a father to the fatherless. After praying, they affirmed that they were beginning to see more and more men visit their home who hadn't had fatherly role models. They seemed encouraged by the word I had shared with them. I was keen to find out more, so I sat down with the man while his wife went to get an after service cup of tea. As soon as we sat down together the man wept and wept. He said to me that what I had shared was particularly pertinent because their own three children had been murdered. All I could do was cry with him. Where do people find hope in the goodness of God when the most horrific things happen in their lives?

I describe the belief that God is good as walking in two countries at the same time: the Kingdom of heaven and the Kingdom of the fallen world. There is a tension between the two. We long and look for the new Kingdom initiated by Jesus and dare to believe that this Kingdom is coming to earth more and more every day through us and God with us. Ultimately, one day this Kingdom will invade earth completely when Jesus returns again.

Don't get me wrong, believing in the goodness of God doesn't mean we sit on our behinds and do nothing. The goodness of God, as revealed through God the Son, shows that this goodness on earth is furthered by taking action. Right at the beginning of his public ministry Jesus declared to his first friends that they should go and do what he did and proclaim that the kingdom of heaven is near - and that they should also have a go at healing the sick while they were about it. "When Jesus had called the Twelve together, he gave them power and authority to drive out demons and to cure diseases, and he sent them out to preach the kingdom of God and to heal the sick." (Luke 9:1-3)

To dare to believe that God is good means we put the belief into action by showing this goodness. The challenge is for us also to take up that charge given to the first friends of Jesus and dramatically show goodness through praying for people and healing them, in Jesus' name.

I always offer to pray for healing for people. My book, *Smack Heads and Fat Cats,* opens with a story of a life changing *Kairos* moment. (A *Kairos* moment is a pivotal time in which you encounter or learn something new about God.) This came about as a result of being panicked so I prayed with a heroin addict who I thought was going to die in front of me. He was completely healed at that very moment. Having had such an experience, I keep on offering to pray for people. Sometimes people agree and seem quite chuffed with the offer. Sometimes people are dramatically healed; other times they aren't. Don't ask me to explain, it just seems to be that in my delight to pray for people, my expectation that something may happen, and my certainty that God does indeed heal, I have found that some are healed while others aren't.

I write that I have an expectation that people will be healed, but to be quite honest there are times when I am surprised that people actually are healed. I went on a prayer walk with one of my friends last year. We ventured off and got somewhat carried away, both in our praying and our walking. A few hours passed, we were in the middle of nowhere; I hadn't packed a picnic and our bellies were rumbling. We thought it a good idea to call in at a pub. So we ventured over a few fields in the vague direction of one to see if it served food. The pub was shut and the landlord, who was outside with his yapping dog, informed us it was closed for the day. We thanked him anyway. He then asked us what we were doing. "Ah, well ... we are on a prayer walk ..." I tried to explain why and that I was a minister, but he still looked at us curiously, as if I had said that we were jelly juggling joggers out for the day, juggling jelly ... as we jogged. We were just about to beat a hasty retreat when I noticed the landlord limping. "What's happened to your leg?" I said. "It's my foot," he explained and pointed to it. "It just swelled up over night and it is really painful, I can hardly walk on it." Before I realised what I was saying, I then offered to pray for him. Eeek! He agreed, so I said a simple prayer asking for the pain to be taken away, that the presence of God would be close to him, and I thanked God for him too. I then said, "I shall keep praying for you, it must be really painful. Sometimes God answers prayers after a while..." The man looked shocked. "Hang on," he said, "this is weird, what did you do? It feels better." He then started walking on it to prove his point. He thanked us and we gently told him that God knew him and that he loved him so much. This man encountered the goodness of God.

God is Father

When he was still a long way off, his father saw him. His heart pounding, he ran out, embraced him, and kissed him. The son started his speech: 'Father, I've sinned against God, I've sinned before you; I don't deserve to be called your son ever again.' But the father wasn't listening. He was calling to the servants, 'Quick. Bring a clean set of clothes and dress him. Put the family ring on his finger and sandals on his feet. Then get a grain-fed heifer and roast it. We're going to feast! We're going to have a wonderful time! My son is here—given up for dead and now alive! Given up for lost and now found!' And they began to have a wonderful time.

(Luke 15:20-24 The Message)

Calling God Father is a bit complicated now-a-days. When I describe God like this to people I just can't help wondering, in the back of my mind, whether their experience of having a dad has been crap. Do we need to take into account the homes where people have had a difficult upbringing, an abusive or over-strict dad or an absent one? How do we talk about God as Father when natural dads may have been the opposite of what God is like?

I believe that, despite the difficulties we and others may have had in our upbringing, we need to believe in God who is Father. Yes, I know Jesus teaches us that God is Spirit and we must worship him in spirit and truth. (John 4:23) Yes, I know that God is like a mother too (Isaiah 66:13), but to say that God is genderless and somehow way beyond being described as a father means we miss out on what it means to have a relationship with a heavenly dad. Just like our beliefs in a God who is love and is good, the belief that he is our Father who longs for his children to be safe and home is one of the most basic characteristic of God, which informs how we then live out being a Christian. You see the God whom we call Father isn't a remote one who watches us on some heavenly CCTV. God walks with each one of us, intimately perceiving how we are, what we are going through, sharing in our joys and struggles. God is with us and I believe he wants us to know and perceive his presence with us more and more.

Furthermore, God is not stagnant. He isn't fossilised for us to study or observe. He grows in relationship with his children - each and every one of the seven billion of them. As Christians we believe that delight in and right-standing with God as Father happens when we believe in Jesus and receive forgiveness. But even then, our relationship with Father God doesn't stand still. He doesn't one day become Father, in a way that means we have immediately learnt and experienced everything about his parenting that we can in our lives. He desires that we get to know more and more of him. There is never a time when we can declare: "Yes, I know everything there is to know. Now ... I'm bored." God as Father desires that people are cared for, that they know that they are known. He longs for people to enjoy his company, to be looked after, and guided in life - to be taught, to be embraced, to be in a vibrant relationship with him. All of that is good news.

If we don't believe God is a loving Father then that will affect our interaction with people around us and hinder our own adventure of being a Christian. When Jesus' first friends asked for a heads-up on how they should pray, the very first words that they were taught were how they should address Almighty God: "Our Father".

This familiarity when addressing God would have been a revelation to those who had many names to describe God, but never called him "Father".

Isaiah prophesied the birth of Jesus some 400 years before the incarnation and he mentioned some names that would be given to him. I find it fascinating that with the birth of the Son, one of the new names would be "Everlasting Father". (Isaiah 9:6) Jesus is the one who reconciles us to God, not in an intangible kind of way, but into a relationship with Dad. Moreover, Paul writes on two occasions (Romans 8:15 and Galatians 4:6) that our new found faith, with the Holy Spirit living in us, means we are now able to cry out "Abba" Father. This title is a tough one to get our heads round: we can now call the creator of the universe, the one who is the very beginning and the end, through whom we have our very being, the one who has given us the very breath we breathe - Daddy.

The importance of this notion of what God is like isn't just for those who do not yet know God as Father. It's also a reminder to Christians that we are brothers and sisters, children of God. It enriches our identity as family. Some of this book was written at a retreat centre run by nuns and a highlight during my week of writing was to join them in their morning and evening prayers. We are the kids of the same dad, and despite our differences we are family. It also gives us, as Christians, the confidence needed to keep going and to know we are not alone. My own journey as a Christian has relied upon this truth. My role as an evangelist over the past 16 years is one that I have pioneered from scratch. The Light Project that I founded has now trained over 120 people in community evangelism, many of whom have received a university degree in the process. We have worked with over 40 different churches to reach out into their communities and bring the good news of Jesus to hundreds of different people week in and week out. Yet it all started with nothing, a faith venture where some months we didn't know whether we would have enough to pay the rent or salaries. So, time and time again, I have had to rely on this most basic fact: that God is my Father. He will provide for me and will lead me. Following where he led, a few years ago I left The Light Project team in Chester in the capable hands of another evangelist and moved to plant the work of gospel sharing in the East of England. I started with a blank canvas. I had to rely on God as my Father to provide for my family and to trust in his guiding and leading to show me what I should do and where to work. Most of the projects that I am involved in now have been ones that I have started up with the express purpose of sharing the gospel with first time hearers. It has been an adventure which I could have never imagined or dreamt. God has given me some of the most beautiful experiences as I seek to further his Kingdom. I share a snippet of my journey with you, not to impress you with how amazing I am, but rather to point to the faithfulness of my Dad. He has done it all. He is my Daddy, and I rely on him for all of my life.

SECTION 2

Big-Hearted Church

Big-Hearted Church

Would Jesus look at the churches all far apart,
And pull them together in the shape of a heart?
from a poem by Lynda Lawson

I'm sitting in the corner of a café people-watching and of particular interest at the moment is a couple at a nearby table. I don't know whether they're married or not, but next to them is a pushchair in which a toddler sleeps while they enjoy their frothy cappuccinos. He's playing with his touchscreen mobile phone, possibly updating his status on a variety of social networks, and she's reading a glossy magazine filled with the latest gossip and numerous photos of celebrities and reality TV stars.

The two of them are about my age, perhaps a bit younger, but as I sit here thinking about next Sunday's sermon, I'm struck once again by the challenge of making the gospel message that means so much to me, relevant not only to this couple, but to the generation to which they belong. I contemplate for a moment my own journey of faith, and am thankful for the experiences that eventually led me to respond to the good news of Jesus Christ. Yet, as my mind wanders back to those few years I spent in Sunday School, the gratitude is mixed with more than a little anger as I remember the day my parents gave up on church.

I'm the eldest of six children, and Sunday mornings were a bit of a nightmare in our household. You can imagine the chaos of getting everyone ready before being squeezed into the car for the short journey across town. We were often late, and on one occasion we were even pulled over by the police for exceeding the speed limit on the way to church! I can assure you that it wasn't the excitement of the service that made us so eager to get there on time – just a desire to avoid the disapproving looks of the congregation as we tried, always unsuccessfully, to take our seats quietly once proceedings had already started.

If I'm honest, by the time I was twelve or thirteen my parents were already being tempted away from the weekly ordeal by the emergence of car boot sales and the allure of a significantly less stressful way to spend a Sunday morning. We were, however, only missing church for one or two services a month, and may well have stayed around longer if it hadn't been for a few careless words uttered on that memorable day. The rest of us went out to Sunday School, but my youngest sister was only a baby at the time and, as there was no crèche facility available, she began to get a bit fidgety during the sermon. When the minister came up to my mother after the service and told her, in no uncertain terms, that she should keep her child quiet or go outside, we left ... and for most of my family, our churchgoing days were over.

Years later I did go back to that church – to lead one of its very last services. In its heyday, the fellowship there had had a real impact on the community in which it was located, but after years of decline the long avoided, but seemingly inevitable decision to close the church had been taken. The sanctuary that had once seated more than three hundred Jesus followers was subsequently sold and is now being used as a Sikh temple.

I thank God for those Sunday School teachers who, week by week, sowed the seeds of faith by introducing me to the stories of Jesus. Unlike my siblings, some sort of connection had remained within me, and during my first week at university, when asked by a member of the Christian Union if I was a believer, I said, "Yes". Thanks to the prayers of my grandmother, an experience of God that I couldn't explain away, and the patience of a guy called Paul Harvey who opened the Bible and challenged me to consider its claims, the Christian faith of my childhood once again became real.

Whilst acknowledging its role in my own salvation, it's my memories of that church, and countless similar congregations that I've heard about and experienced over the years, that begin to irritate me as I look down and realise that my latte is now cold. If the couple I've been watching give any thought to the church, which is unlikely, what passes through their mind is probably going to be negative. So what is it that caused a life-changing and world-transforming movement, initiated by

God's powerful Spirit at a Pentecost gathering in Jerusalem two thousand years ago, to turn into the often immovable institution that exists today? Where did we get the idea that the church is called to maintain faithfully the traditions of previous generations at the expense of finding fresh and relevant ways to proclaim the good news of Jesus Christ and bear the fruit of the kingdom in this, our generation?

I love the church, and it's because it means so much to me that I feel angry about the way many congregations have allowed themselves to become outdated and unrelated to the lives of people like the couple who are now getting ready to leave. He's finished his social networking, but his spiritual need to belong and to connect to something bigger than himself remains unmet. She's devoured most of the magazine, but the deep desire for her own life to have significance and purpose is still unsatisfied. Into the spiritual vacuum left by the retreating church all manner of empty promises are being made, and broken. The need for a Saviour is as real now as it has ever been, and those of us who, like me, have heard and embraced the gospel, have the joyful responsibility of sharing it with others.

The two lines of verse that opened this section of the book were part of a poem written by a new church member and given to me as a gift recently. I love the wonderful picture it paints on the canvas of my imagination – a heart-shaped church! Over the years, cathedrals and churches have been laid out in the shape of a cross, a reminder of that great act of love at the centre of the gospel message, but I wonder if there has ever been one designed in the shape of a heart?

Clearly, however, my friend Lynda wasn't thinking of a church building at all. Although she only recently became a Christian, the questions she asks me about Jesus have illustrated a deeper understanding of what the church is. To imagine a heart-shaped church is not the work of an architect, but a challenge for God's people to rediscover the big-heart of our God and to allow that discovery to transform the way we gather together and live out our faith in the places that we work and play. That is what this part of the book is all about, and whilst I offer the disclaimer that neither I, nor RE:NEW (the church to which I currently belong), are yet particularly *big-hearted*, I know that I was invited by Chris to write this section because in some small way we have, as a community, been trying to work out what being *big-hearted* means, and seeking, step by step, to put it into practice.

Whilst I am hopeful that the thoughts offered in these pages will be relevant to you, whatever part of the family of God you belong to, I write as a Baptist minister, and from within the context of that denomination. Indeed, the chapters that follow are based upon the five core values that came out of a consultation within the Baptist Union of Great Britain back in 1996[6]. As I re-examined these values from a big-hearted perspective, however, I was once again struck by the way that these ideals define who we are, not by what separates us from other denominations, but by what unites us with them.

This unity has been an important strand throughout the short life of RE:NEW, and a brief portion of our imperfect and continuing story concludes each of the chapters in this section. But these values are not original or innovative; they've been expressed throughout the history of the church, and within our shared heritage are those individuals and groups who seem to have embodied them in a particularly powerful way. The title of this book was itself inspired by a phrase used to describe one of these people, St. Francis of Assisi, whose ministry was characterised by "simple words but largeness of heart"[7], and each of the following chapters opens with a short episode from his story.

As you read I ask that you join me in a prayer for congregations across this land to embrace these values. Dream of yourself, and those you meet with Sunday by Sunday, living them out and making them a priority in all that you do. See in your mind's eye the walls of your church building becoming as transparent as glass, with the people inside being drawn towards, and then being enveloped, into a huge red heart. Then imagine that heart, of which you are now a part, expanding so much that it breaks down the walls and soon fills the whole of your neighbourhood. God longs for his big-heart to be made visible, and he invites the church to join willingly with him in his big-hearted mission to the world. And as we do so, who knows what incredible things might happen?

Value 1: The Big-Hearted Church is a Gospel Telling Community

How, then, can they call on the one they have not believed in?
And how can they believe in the one of whom they have not heard?
And how can they hear without someone preaching to them?
And how can they preach unless they are sent?
(Romans 10:14-15)

Big-Hearted Heritage – Part 1

One day early in 1205, as Francis sat through the mass, he became troubled by the gospel reading which described how Christ had sent his disciples out to share the good news of the kingdom. After the service he went and asked the priest to explain it to him, and after he had done so the young man, moved by the Spirit of God, exclaimed: "This is what I have needed, this is what I have searched for, this is what I long to do with all my heart." From then on, with an overflowing joy, Francis committed himself to the word of God and to putting it into practice in his life. With great fervour he began to preach, and all were amazed and challenged by his simple words but largeness of heart.[8]

As a child I used to suffer from asthma; perhaps you did too, or maybe you know someone who had the condition. If you've ever seen or experienced an asthma attack you will know that it suddenly becomes very difficult to breathe. It feels as if you can't get enough air into your lungs and you end up gasping – taking lots of in-breaths but not being able to breathe out properly.

As I've reflected on the variety of churches that I've been part of and visited over the years, I've come to the conclusion that some of them have been suffering from asthma too! To stay alive an organism needs to breathe – in and out, in and out – and the church, the body of Christ, is no different. The church breathes in the Spirit of God as it gathers together in the name of Jesus, and breathes out the Holy Spirit as it engages in mission, going out into the world to tell others the good news of the kingdom. But somewhere along the line we started gasping – in, in, in – and for some reason forgot that we needed to breathe out too!

If my doctor wanted to assess how bad my asthma was at a particular point in time he would ask me to blow into a peak-flow meter. This little device would monitor my ability to breathe out and determine whether my health was improving or not. In my role as a minister, and as a mission consultant, I've often thought that it would be great if there was something similar to measure a congregation's gospel telling capacity. There are, however, a few general observations we can make to get a good idea.

1) Have a look through your church events diary for the next month or so. How many of the activities listed here are taking place either *in* the church building or *in* the home of one of the church members? Are there any events that are scheduled to take place *out* in the community: at the local school, at the pub or maybe at the park?

2) What are the explicit and implicit expectations of the minister? Are most of their weekly tasks focused on meeting the needs of those *in* the church? Or have they been released to spend a good amount of their time in activities such as chaplaincy in the local care home, leading lessons and assemblies in the local school or even serving on its governing body? Are leaders supported in their efforts to make evangelism a high priority, or is their task seen, first and foremost, as pastoral?

3) How about the members of the church? Are they actively encouraged to participate in local community groups and serve on the parish council? Or are there disapproving looks when their choice to fulfil these

responsibilities occasionally clash with a church meeting or Bible study group? How willing are people to take risks for the sake of the gospel – for example, by offering prayers for healing on the local High Street?

As an asthma sufferer I didn't try to convince my doctor that it wasn't necessary to breathe out. In the same way most churches don't need persuading that mission should be an integral part of church life. The trouble is that many congregations equate mission with the church *growing* rather than it *going*! What they want are more people to *come* to the church, mistakenly thinking that Jesus' words in Matthew 28:19 were the "Great *Come*-Mission", rather than remembering that this verse starts with the word: "Go". Don't get me wrong here, a healthy church – one that is breathing properly – will grow. In my experience, however, there are plenty of churches who say that they want to grow, and pray earnestly that they would grow, and yet, when the Lord asks them to "go", they refuse. Throughout the Bible, those to whom God has revealed his big-heart have usually been sent to share it with others:

- Moses – "The cry of the Israelites has reached me, and I have seen the way the Egyptians are oppressing them. So now, **go**." (Exodus 3:9-10)

- Isaiah – "Whom shall I send? And who will **go** for us?" (Isaiah 6:8)

- Jeremiah – "**Go** to everyone I send you to and say whatever I command you." (Jeremiah 1:7)

- The Disciples – "After this the Lord appointed seventy-two others and sent them two by two ahead of him to every town and place where he was about to go. He told them… '**Go!**'" (Luke 10:1-3)

Just in case we think these people were in some way special – the Biblical equivalents of missionaries, those people in our churches who are called to go and share the gospel abroad – the Baptist Union of Great Britain recently adopted the tagline "Encouraging Missionary Disciples". The vision and strategy encapsulated in these words is not to persuade more church members to get on a plane and fly across the world (although some may indeed hear such a call); rather it's a rallying cry for churches to rediscover the Biblical imperative to _go_: to leave behind the comforts of the traditional and the familiar, and to go into their communities and share God's big-heart with them in a language that they will understand.

The publication of the Church of England document _Mission-Shaped Church_[9] was a similar reminder that the church "exists to serve and to participate in the ongoing mission of God"[10]. It recognised, at the outset, the major ways in which society had changed, and identified the need for the church to respond appropriately to the dramatically new situation that we find ourselves in. Stuart Murray, a Baptist theologian who is quoted in the report, goes so far as saying that our culture is experiencing a "paradigm shift" between "Christendom and ... post-Christendom"[11]. Imagine being a Christian in the year 312AD; recently persecuted as a minority movement within the Roman Empire, and then suddenly part of a religious institution endorsed by Emperor Constantine after his own dramatic conversion. The challenge we face now is just as significant, only in the opposite direction. Whilst society has been undergoing such considerable change, many congregations have preserved their status quo, or made only minor adjustments to what they do. A recent survey reveals the result – two thirds of the UK population now "have no connection with church".[12] Half of these have never been in touch with a church, whilst the other half, for one reason or another, have given up coming.[13]

It's not that churches have stopped preaching the gospel; it's just that those who need to hear the good news aren't within earshot! Faced with this reality we have to decide which we want more – for the kingdom to thrive or for our particular congregation to survive. We can either take the risk of going to where the people are and changing the shape of what we do so that it is fit for the purpose of mission or we can doggedly maintain what exists for as long as we can, and keep hoping that people will come. This second option could, I suppose, be called "church-shaped mission", where the missionary task of the congregation is fashioned around and fitted into the existing patterns of church, rather than the other way around.

Of course, one of the main reasons people resist change is that they fear losing something which is of great value to them. Whilst this is understandable, the gospel is quite clear about the cost of being a missionary disciple: "I tell you, unless a kernel of wheat falls to the ground and dies, it remains only a single seed. But if it dies, it produces many seeds. Those who love their life will lose it, while those who hate their life in this world will keep it for eternal life."[14] If we are willing to take these words of Jesus seriously we must be prepared, for the sake of the gospel, to allow old patterns of church practice to die in order for the new to emerge. In *Mission-Shaped Church*, as its authors reflect upon the big-heart of God expressed in the death of Jesus upon the cross, it too concludes that:

> "If it is the nature of God's love to undertake such sacrifice, it must also be the nature of his Church. The Church is most true to itself when it gives itself up, in current cultural form, to be re-formed among those who do not know God's Son. In each new context the Church must die to live."[15]

Clearly the incarnation is central to the gospel message – out of God's great love for humanity "the Word became flesh and made his dwelling among us". (John 1:14) In Jesus the big-heart of God became accessible in the context of first century Palestine, and it is this reality that "the church is called upon to proclaim afresh in each generation".[16] Many congregations can look back with pride over decades and even centuries of faithful ministry, but sometimes, somewhere along the line, a church can forget who and what it is called to be. Some fellowships give the impression that their primary duty is not to the church as an incarnation of God's love, but rather to the church as an institution charged with the task of preserving the customs and practices it has accumulated over the years. When we realise that we are first and foremost stewards of the gospel, we become free to find new and culturally relevant ways to tell the wonderful news to a generation that is yet to hear it.

Big-Hearted Beginners – Part 1

In early 2006 the 20 or so members of the Lode Chapel fellowship were preparing for the summer holiday Bible club that it organised every two years at the primary school in Bottisham, the largest of the local villages and the natural hub of the rural community situated to the north-east of Cambridge. The club had been a regular and well attended feature of the church's outreach for a number of years. In the past, however, despite positive contact being made during the week with a large number of the families, there had been very little follow-up to the club. This matter was raised at one of our regular meetings with the local Anglican vicar and we ended up talking about the possibility of holding a monthly "holiday club on a Sunday". It was interesting, given subsequent events, that the idea arose in this context, but after initial discussions it began as just a Lode Chapel activity. At a church meeting the congregation agreed to give up its usual Sunday morning service in the Chapel once a month and so, in September 2006, "Sunday Club" was born. There were personal invitations for the children who had been to the holiday club, and adverts in the village magazines and through the schools. Just like a holiday club, the morning involved video, games, craft, action songs, a creative prayer activity and a short talk focused around a memory verse. A number of families joined us at the first event and although a few didn't return, some continued to come month by month. The hard work put into preparing each event, including transporting the newly purchased sound and video equipment to and from the school, seemed to be bearing fruit.

Value 2: The Big-Hearted Church is a Gospel Dwelling Community

As you come to him, the living Stone –rejected by men but chosen by God and precious to him –you also, like living stones, are being built into a spiritual house. (1 Peter 2:4-5)

Big-Hearted Heritage – Part 2

In the autumn of that same year Francis had gone to meditate in the fields when he saw the old and dilapidated church of St. Damian and was prompted by the Spirit to go and pray within it. As he prostrated himself in prayer before an image of Christ on the cross he was moved to tears. He looked up at Jesus and heard an audible voice saying three times to him: "Francis, go and repair my house, which, as you can see, is falling utterly into ruin." Being alone in the church, and experiencing such ecstasy in his heart, he knew that God had spoken to him. After some time he got up and committed himself to repairing the church in which he stood. Later, upon completing the task, the Holy Spirit helped him to realise that the main purpose of the message had not been about the building, but about the Church that Christ had purchased by his blood.[17]

It's a well-worn cliché, but it's true – "The church is the people and not the building." Very few believers will openly disagree with the statement, but try asking them to start meeting somewhere else on a Sunday morning, and you'll find it's certainly not that simple! Anyone who's been part of a church that's removed pews or had any sort of refurbishment will know just how attached some people can be to the physical place that they gather in week by week. A friend of mine ministered in a church with a moveable pulpit, but when she suggested its relocation to a more convenient spot at the front of the sanctuary, a few people strongly objected. More pastorally sensitive than I, this minister decided to implement such a radical change in smaller, more manageable steps, and each Sunday, literally inch by inch, slowly but surely, the pulpit arrived in its new position.

The second value of a big-hearted church is to be a prophetic, or gospel-dwelling, community. Our words, our actions and our priorities, whether we like it or not, are all ways in which the watching world understands the Christian faith. It's true that God communicates with people in all sorts of *sacred spaces*, but if we become too pre-occupied with our church buildings then we are in danger of giving the impression that bricks and mortar are more important to us, and by implication God, than the joys and sorrows of people's daily lives. We all know that this isn't true, but from the number of times I've heard people refer to the church building as "the house of God", I do think we need to clarify our thinking.

Part of the problem is that we've slipped back into an Old Testament temple mentality. When we read the story of Solomon building the temple in Jerusalem and of Ezra restoring it, we note that the glory of God was visibly present above the Ark of the Covenant in the Holy of Holies. The religious activities and festivities of God's people were therefore focused around the temple, and it had great significance for them. But, as the author of Hebrews explains[18], the tearing of the curtain at the moment of Jesus' death[19] made temple worship redundant. No longer would buildings be the residing place of the divine – God's people themselves would be his dwelling[20]. When the Spirit fills the disciples on Pentecost, a new pattern of worship begins to take shape:

"They devoted themselves to the apostles' teaching and to the fellowship, to the breaking of bread and to prayer. Everyone was filled with awe, and many wonders and miraculous signs were done by the apostles. All the believers were together and had everything in common. Selling their possessions and goods, they gave to anyone as he had need. Every day they continued to meet together in the temple courts. They broke bread in their

homes and ate together with glad and sincere hearts."
(Acts 2:43-46)

There are a couple of important themes to highlight here.
Firstly, note the way that, just as it had been throughout
Jesus' ministry, the gospel continues to be proclaimed both in
word and deed. The teaching of the apostles, the evidence of
the miracles (John 14:12) and the ethical nature of the
Christian community are all distinctive aspects of their public
witness in the temple courts. Secondly, we also see them
gathering in their homes to eat together and break bread in
remembrance of the one in whose name they met. (Luke
22:19) If we go back to the breathing analogy used in the last
chapter, what we can observe here is a balance between the
out and *in* movements of the early church.

But let's think a bit more about the nature of the disciples'
activity in the temple courts: why are they here if the temple
is no longer the dwelling place of God? Was the building still
necessary for them to meet with him, or is there some other
reason for their presence in this place? Look, for example, at
the story of the man who begged at the Beautiful Gate in Acts
3. We don't see Peter and John going to a prayer meeting
tucked away in a private room within the temple precincts,
but rather, I would suggest, two disciples choosing an ideal
time and place to share the gospel with those who are yet to
believe. If we get the impression that this is somehow
equivalent to healing a man who, being homeless and sat on

the church steps, was invited to join the worship service, then we've missed the point. A better way to understand this would be to think about a small group of Christians heading down to the local High Street when it was at its busiest, praying for people there, and then engaging with the passers-by who have stopped to see what all the fuss is about.

As time goes on, however, don't we see the Jewish disciples continuing to attend synagogue? Well, if we have a look at the passages in which we are told that Paul and the others went to the synagogue[21] we can see the sole purpose of their attendance was to reason with and persuade the Jews that Jesus was the Messiah. When the Jews refuse to listen they stop going to the synagogue and instead go to the marketplace or to the places where open debates were taking place. Although we might call our Sunday morning gatherings acts of *public* worship, haven't we lost sight of what we see in scripture, and so they are, in practice, mostly preaching to the already converted?

Many congregations today will have house groups of one sort or another – and these are perhaps more comparable to the times when the early churches would gather together for prayer, for teaching and discussion from scripture, for singing, and for sharing meals and breaking bread[22]. This *in* activity is vitally important, which is why the writer of Hebrews says: "Let us not give up meeting together, as some are in the habit of doing." (Hebrews 10:25) In many churches, however, whether the people are gathering on a Sunday or midweek, the inward focus is usually the same, and the *in-out* balance, evident in the pattern of life for the early believers, has been lost.

It's not that our church buildings aren't necessary or useful. Indeed, some of them have become so well used by the local community that during the week they provide an ideal place to meet individuals and share the gospel with them. The trouble comes when we imagine that the only way people will have an encounter with God is by them entering "his house" on a Sunday morning. This mistakenly reinstates the temple worship that was so powerfully and visibly done away with on Good Friday when the curtain was torn in two. If we realise once again that it's the people of God who are his dwelling, then we become free to treat our church buildings simply as one more resource in the task of living out the gospel.

A gospel-dwelling church understands that if it is fulfilling the prophetic task, our friends and neighbours will more readily identify us with the good news of the kingdom than with a particular building or organisation. This is not just the gospel that we proclaim with our lips, but also the message heard loud and clear through what we do and how we live. If we and our churches have come under the lordship of Christ, then this will be evident in the way we relate to one another, and to those in need. Whilst at some point we will need to explain in words what the gospel is, the opportunities to do this will arise when people are able to see it in action in our lives.

For this to be true of us two things are required. The first is that we, individually and corporately, continually need to seek to apply the word of God, and the distinctive ethics of the kingdom of God, to the particular moral challenges of our time. How can we appropriately engage with injustice and inequality? How can we play our part in addressing the issue of climate change? What should our response be to powerful influences of consumerism and individualism? The second prophetic requirement is that we get out of our church buildings a bit more and enter the public arena so that people can see our lives and hear our voices.

Big-Hearted Beginners – Part 2

During 2007 a new curate and his wife arrived in the Anglican Benefice serving the same rural community as Lode Chapel. Soon after this, one of the parish churches agreed to resource an event similar to "Sunday Club" in another of the local schools. Both eventually adopted the new name of "RE:NEW", and the same ecumenical planning team was involved in organising these two "fresh expressions" of church. Although some of the events encouraged all ages to participate together, generally the children continued to enjoy the holiday club format whilst the adults met separately in a café style atmosphere with coffee, cake, newspapers, video and discussion.

The numbers of those attending rose and fell, but notably there were a few regular families who previously had little or no contact with the church. A couple of years later, however, when it became clear that the curate would be moving on, the story of RE:NEW reached a crossroads. The second event relocated back to the parish church as a monthly all-age "Good News" service, and our fellowship began to discuss what its next step should be. The congregation had been disappointed at the way the RE:NEW families were not then coming to other services at Lode Chapel, and slowly it became apparent that God was calling us to "go" to them.

After three church meetings in five weeks, at which people had been free to share their hopes and fears, it was time to make the final decision. When it was clear that those present were unanimous in their support to move our Sunday morning services to the school, one of the young people (who had been involved in the discussions) exclaimed "It's a miracle!" – and indeed it was. So on Sunday 14 February 2010, the same date that we celebrated 200 years since the purchase of the land on which the Chapel was built, we held a special service to announce the fact that: "The church had left the building!" We've gathered ecumenically as RE:NEW at the school almost every Sunday since.

Value 3: The Big-Hearted Church is a Generously Giving Community

Remember this: Whoever sows sparingly will also reap
sparingly,
and whoever sows generously will also reap generously...
God loves a cheerful giver and... is able to make all grace
abound to you, so that in all things
at all times, having all that you need, you will abound in every
good work.
(2 Corinthians 9:6,8)

Big-Hearted Heritage – Part 3

Before fully understanding the meaning of the command to "repair my house" Francis set about the task of restoring the building in which God had spoken to him. He gathered what possessions he could and went immediately to the city of Foligno where he sold all of the goods that he had brought, and even the horse he had ridden to get there. Francis returned on foot to Assisi and entered the church of St. Damian, and on finding the priest there, he offered him all of the money for the repair of the church and the use of the poor.

The father of Francis, upon hearing what his son had done, was incensed and took him before the bishop of the city, hoping to reclaim all that had been given away. Francis was unrepentant but was nonetheless willing to give back all that he still had – so he removed the clothes he was wearing, including his underwear, and presented them to his father. Standing naked he said: "Until now I have called you my father, but from now on I confidently declare that my treasure rests with 'Our Father in heaven' in whom I place complete trust and hope." The bishop, seeing this and marvelling at such commitment to Christ, got up and weeping put his arms around Francis before using his own cloak to cover his nakedness.[23]

In this story, St. Francis demonstrates the same joyful abandon suggested by Jesus when he says: "If someone wants to sue you and take your tunic, let him have your cloak as well." (Matthew 5:40) I guess some people will be offended at the way the zealous young man took this passage to the extreme as he stripped naked in front of his father and the bishop, but sometimes in church our desire for respectability and propriety can quench the spirit of cheerful generosity. In the face of such criticism Francis may well have used the words first spoken by David; responding to Michal's reprimand about his leaping and dancing the king replies: "I will become even more undignified than this!" (2 Samuel 6:22)

The third core value suggested by the Baptist Union describes the church as a "sacrificial community". Whilst this phrase adequately expresses our desire to imitate Christ, and the way that he laid down his life on our behalf, it somehow lacks the sense of the big-heart about it. The term "generously giving" perhaps more fully encapsulates the spirit in which the New Testament urges us to offer ourselves, and all that we have, as we participate in the coming of the kingdom. My wife was born in the West Indies, and if you've ever been in an Afro-Caribbean congregation you may well have experienced the energetic and joyful attitude that many of these churches have when it comes to donating to the Lord's work. There is no need for the offering to be *taken*, a word that is often heard elsewhere; rather, it is willingly and cheerfully given as the people leave their seats and practically dance down the aisle, waving their gifts in the air and singing as they go. It's not that their gifts aren't costly, they often are, but as well as the sacrifice there is also much gladness. In our situation we may, for example, have to endure the pain of giving up the traditions that we value so much, in order to experience the joy of bringing others to Christ.

In the introduction to this section of the book I explained that I made my own commitment to Christ whilst at university. As graduation approached I sensed a strong call to give a year of voluntary work to the church of which I had become a part. It was a small congregation and although it had a minister, it had no spare funds with which to support me, and that year became my first experience of *living by faith*. It's still hard to explain how I managed to pay for accommodation and food and everything else, but somehow, by the end of the year I had not only survived, but had also managed to pay off the overdraft with which I had left university! Occasionally an envelope of cash would drop anonymously on to my doorstep, but just like the Biblical account of the five loaves and two fish[24], no matter how little there was to start with, there always seemed to be enough, with some left over.

As a congregation too we learned to trust in God's provision. Being a city centre church we could literally see the issue of homelessness right on our doorstep, and felt called to do something in response. We explored the possibility of transforming part of the premises into a night shelter, but soon realised that the cost of this building work would be in the region of £180,000. After further number crunching we realised that it would cost a similar amount each year to run the shelter with appropriately trained staff and volunteers. With a membership of just over 30, mainly elderly, people it was beyond us! But nonetheless we stepped out in faith, and the result – food and accommodation for more than two dozen people every single night of the year –

became a clear demonstration that: "Nothing is impossible with God." (Luke 1:37)

For us to be generous givers, as individuals and as churches, we first need to understand the generosity of God. The verses at the opening of this chapter are taken from a passage in which Paul focuses on the issue of giving.[25] Like the church in Corinth, we need constant reminding that the resources of God never run short and that, when we are living in obedience to him, he will supply all of our needs. In these verses[26] Paul refers to the provision of manna for Israel as they wandered in the wilderness – each family had enough, but only just enough, to meet their daily needs. It was therefore necessary to trust God for the needs of tomorrow. Paul's words, along with Moses' prohibition on hoarding the manna (except ahead of the Sabbath), can make difficult reading for those churches accumulating or sitting on a healthy reserve in their bank accounts. Such churches miss out on the excitement of living by faith and witnessing for themselves God's gracious provision, as well as the blessings that come when we generously share what we have with others.

The model that we see Paul advocating to the Corinthian church is simply an expansion to the congregational level of the individual believers having "everything in common". (Acts 2:44) In a world where being independent is often lauded as a virtue, God's people are called to be dependent upon God and interdependent upon one another. Churches need to live in loving relationships with one another, and as they do so they will become channels through which the resources of God can be given and received. Whilst Paul uses the analogy of sowing and reaping, I've found another helpful metaphor in a book entitled *The Soul of Money*. Here is what the author, Lynne Twist, learned from a poor elderly lady she met in a church basement in Harlem:

> "Gertrude taught me that money is like water. Money flows through all our lives, sometimes like a rushing river, and sometimes like a trickle. When it is flowing, it can purify, cleanse, create growth, and nourish. But when it is blocked or held too long, it can grow stagnant and toxic to those withholding or hoarding it... We can be flooded with money and drown in its excess, and when we dam it up unnecessarily, we keep it out of circulation to the detriment of others."[27]

As disciples of Jesus we are people who have freely received the riches of heaven, and we are called to give just as freely for the sake of the kingdom. (Matthew 10:8) This is seen not just in our support of fellow Christians in this country and overseas, but through the missionary task within our own communities. I've seen a few church budgets over the years and it is surprising how often there is nothing, or only a very small amount, set aside for local mission. Spending money on church buildings and a minister, but not budgeting for mission is like owning a car and employing a driver, but refusing to buy any petrol!

A community should be blessed by the presence of a church in its midst, but sometimes the people living nearby are indifferent or even negative towards the congregation (remembering only the last contact they had with the church which may well have been a request to donate to its latest building project). When Jesus visited a town or a village he healed the sick, fed the hungry, turned water into wine, or left some other sign of God's unconditional love for the people who lived there. As we see in the story of the healing of the ten lepers, when only one returned to thank Jesus (Luke 17:11-19), such acts will not always result in an immediate response to the gospel, but we are nonetheless called to imitate Christ faithfully in generously sharing God's big-heart for the neighbourhoods in which we live and work.

Being an individual or a church which takes up the challenge to be generous givers is not without cost. Indeed, as we see at the cross, sometimes it can cost the giver everything – but that isn't a reason not to give. In this particular era during the history of the church in this country there are some powerful stories of costly generosity. Take, for example, the Methodist church near the beach at Polzeath in Cornwall where the few remaining members decided to stop holding traditional services and hand over their chapel (worth millions in real estate) so that it could be used to reach out to the next generation. Although that old fellowship is no more, the building is now the home of a thriving church which reaches out to the young surfers and skateboarders who gather nearby. There are a growing number of similar stories of dying churches generously giving up their own existence to bring forth new life in the body of Christ – what better way to illustrate the powerful message of sacrifice and hope at the heart of our Christian faith!

Big-Hearted Beginners – Part 3

In addition to the school-based gatherings on Sunday mornings, RE:NEW has organised a variety of community blessing events and activities. One weekend we hired a bouncy castle and inflated it in the local park; whilst the children leaped about to their hearts' content, the adults enjoyed freshly made bacon sandwiches. On another occasion we had a communal excursion to IKEA – with RE:NEW hiring a large van to bring back all of the furniture that people couldn't fit into their cars. We've also organised a few community car washes, with coffee and cake provided whilst people wait for their car to be ready. My ordination service, which was held in the school in 2008, at the end of another holiday Bible club, was also an opportunity to give generously to the community. There was face-painting for all of the children who came along, as well as a barbeque and an ice-cream vendor offering on the house as much of my favourite food as people could eat. One thing in common across all of these and other events is that they were offered completely free of charge – and this fact is always noted by those who benefit from them.

But generosity is not always financial. Towards the end of the first year at the school we reviewed the move to decide whether to stay there or to return to the chapel. As the review approached, three ladies in the congregation, who had all struggled with the new surroundings, told me of their desire to go back to the way things were. They also told me, however, that they were praying about the decision, and subsequently each of them, in different ways, individually heard from God that it was right for us to stay. Their willingness to submit to God's will, rather than acting upon their own will, was a powerful testimony of God's guidance, and one of the most generous acts I have ever seen in a church context.

Value 4: The Big-Hearted Church is a Grace Growing Community

The grace of our Lord was poured out on me abundantly, along with the faith and love that are in Christ Jesus. Here is a trustworthy saying that deserves full acceptance: Christ Jesus came into the world to save sinners – of whom I am the worst. But for that very reason I was shown mercy so that in me, the worst of sinners, Christ Jesus might display his unlimited patience as an example for those who would believe on him and receive eternal life.

(1 Timothy 1:14-16)

Big-Hearted Heritage – Part 4

Before his conversion Francis had been known to mock those who suffered with leprosy: looking in the direction of their house, which was still two miles away, he had held his nose as if the smell offended him. But now, as he began to grow in grace and in the power of God, upon meeting lepers God would enable him to go near them and greet them with a kiss. Indeed, Francis, filled with compassion, would often visit their homes in order to wash them and carefully cleanse the ulcers that covered their skin.[28]

Over the years many people joined Francis and some of these brothers set up a leper hospital. On one occasion, when Francis was visiting, he encountered a patient who constantly blasphemed and was violent and abusive to all who had tried to serve him. Francis prayed for the man and then, after greeting him, he asked what could be done. "Wash me all over," the man said, "for I am so disgusting that I cannot bear myself." Miraculously, as Francis washed the man, his leprosy was healed and he began to weep bitterly and repent of his sins. [29]

A reawakening to the reality of saving grace was one of the key factors in the Reformation, but it seems to me that we constantly need to rediscover and realign ourselves with the amazing and sometimes unsettling nature of God's love for humanity. When I talk to people about why they don't go to church, or why they have stopped going, they will often tell me a story that is characterised by a distinct lack of grace. Those who are a decade or two older than I recount tales of churches that have tied up the swings in the local playground so that children couldn't play on Sundays, or of people who have been reprimanded by the elders of the church for going to the cinema. Those who are parents now tell me stories of being made to feel unwelcome because their young children wouldn't sit quietly during prayers, or having been sternly told off by the church secretary because there was a bit of play dough stuck to the carpet after toddler group one week.

An expanded definition of the Greek word *charis*, which is translated in the New Testament as "grace", says the following: "graciousness... especially the divine influence upon the heart, and its reflection in the life".[30] Those of us who are recipients of God's grace are called to reflect this in the gracious way we relate to others. Maybe this is what the Baptist Union is referring to in the fourth of its five core values, where it suggests that we are to be an "inclusive community". At first glance, inclusivity is easy to define – it's about being welcoming no matter what a person's age, ethnic background, disability or social status. Beyond that point, however, it gets more complicated and controversial. Are we pushing inclusivity too far by insisting that leadership roles are equally accessible to both women and men? And how can we be inclusive of those whose lifestyles we find at odds with our understanding of Scripture?

Whilst these questions do need to be wrestled with, I think it is more helpful for us to describe this value in terms of us being "grace growing" communities. I can't remember who first introduced me to this expression, but it was at a time when there was someone in my life who was particularly irritating and quite frequently offensive. The wise, yet sadly forgotten, friend described this person as my "grace grower" and suggested that my relationship with him was an opportunity to nurture this most vital of Christian virtues. A fresh outlook on my situation enabled me to forgive my tormentor, and within this new atmosphere of grace he also began to change in attitude and behaviour.

The reality of our fallen world is that it is, at times, a little bit messy – and it's tempting to make the church a tidy little refuge where those who belong, or want to belong, are required to behave in a certain way. When this happens the church is in danger of becoming a place populated by people who wear a mask of respectability at the expense of honesty and accountability. Within such a congregation people can become fearful of sharing their struggles, and people outside the church get the impression that they need to get their lives sorted out before even crossing the threshold. The result is a *virtual holiness* and the church ceases to be a community into which real people are invited to experience the healing and transforming love of God.

A church that is growing in grace will also be able to embrace people who believe differently. Whilst it is important to be clear on the fundamentals of the faith as expressed in the historic creeds, a healthy church will nonetheless welcome doubt and debate about the non-essentials. The trouble is that many church leaders feel so threatened by diversity that they often develop a long list of beliefs to help their church define who is *in* and who is *out*. The danger of being focused on the boundary of the church, however, is that we all too easily lose sight of the centre. Rather than *in-or-out* churches, we are called to be *in-and-out* communities of missionary disciples who, as they focus upon Jesus, point others in his direction. One author, Richard Thomas, describes this type of church as "a set of people who have a connection to Christ ... moving towards the free, beautiful, compassionate spirit of Christ, which they have made the centre of their lives".[31] Imagine how powerful the witness would be if a congregation was distinctive, not for a particular set of beliefs that set it apart from the church down the road, but for its abundant reservoirs of grace.

To be a church of grace growers requires believers who see faith as a journey. Like the prodigal son (Luke 15:11-32), some may become aware of their sin when they are a long way off; but, whatever state our lives are in when this happens, it is that moment of turning towards Jesus, and asking him for his help and forgiveness, which marks the start of our journey home. When the purpose of a church is to help everyone move closer to the centre, people will be graciously welcomed no matter where they are on the journey, and always encouraged to follow wherever Christ is leading them next.

As well as nurturing grace within the church, however, we are also called to the task of grace growing within our communities. This "ministry of reconciliation" (2 Corinthians 5:18) will not always be an easy one, and we may sometimes even become unpopular as we reach out to those whom other people prefer to push to the margins. One powerful example of this made the headlines in 2003 when a rector intervened in an angry and venomous exchange between the settled residents of the Cambridgeshire village of Cottenham and the travelling community who lived at the nearby Smithy Fen[32]. Slowly, but surely, in a long process that sought to encourage a constructive dialogue between the two groups, Rev. Michael Hore helped them to understand each other's hopes and fears.

Over the centuries there have been periods in the life of the church when grace has been in short supply. Indeed, we've sometimes been more like the religious authorities who persecuted Jesus for his association with the "tax collectors and 'sinners'",[33] rather than seeking to imitate our Saviour who was so graciously able to challenge people about their sin without condemning them in the process.[34] In Acts 15, during one of the first recorded meetings of the early church, we witness the disciples also struggling to get the balance right. The Gentiles were starting to believe in Jesus, and to be filled with the Holy Spirit, and some of the Jewish believers were keen for these new converts to maintain the status quo. As we seek to be inclusive churches, however, we would do well to listen to the conclusions of the Jerusalem Council: "We believe it is through the grace of our Lord Jesus that we are saved, just as they are," (Acts 15:11) and therefore: "We should not make it difficult for [those] who are turning to God." (Acts 15:19)

Big-Hearted Beginners – Part 4

As new individuals and families got more and more involved in the life of RE:NEW it was important, at the appropriate time, for us to encourage them in their commitment to Christ, and to the community of which they were becoming a part. But questions arose within the fellowship about whether more than a declaration of believing faith in Christ was required by those seeking to participate fully in the life of the church. Were certain standards of behaving (for example marriage rather than cohabitation) also necessary before people were permitted to belong? The following statement is what we agreed:

A person becomes a member of the body of Christ when their heart is first turned towards God and they take their first steps on a journey of faith. This spiritual reality is expressed publicly through baptism and through ongoing active participation in a local congregation – and this is what is meant by church membership. The implication is that the local church is made up of believers who have chosen, for a period of time, to walk together in their individual journeys of faith. Some believers will have just started their journey; others will have been on a journey of faith for many years. Some believers will have evidence of God's redeeming work in many aspects of their lives; in the lives of others only the first fruits of this redeeming work will be evident. Nonetheless, it is our belief that God works through his Spirit which is powerfully present in the church, and all those who publicly express their belief in Christ, have started on a journey of faith, and seek to grow spiritually, will be welcomed as part of the church, and are invited to become partners in its ministry and mission.

Value 5: The Big-Hearted Church is a Glory Glowing Community

I will extol the Lord at all times;
his praise will always be on my lips.
My soul will boast in the Lord;
let the afflicted hear and rejoice.
Glorify the Lord with me; let us exalt his name together.
I sought the Lord, and he answered me; he delivered me from
all my fears.
Those who look to him are radiant.
(Psalms 34:1-5)

Big-Hearted Heritage – Part 5

Although always mindful of the task of mission, Francis would nonetheless often seek out solitary places so that he could turn his attentions completely towards God. Whether he was walking, sitting, eating or drinking, he sought to do all things in communion with the divine, but it was when he was alone with God that he received the grace to overcome the fears and temptations which afflicted him. Doing only what the Lord prompted he preached to thousands as confidently as if he were talking to a close friend and to individuals with the care of one who speaks to the multitude.

On a visit to Rome, he was initially apprehensive about addressing the Pope and the cardinals. As he stood up, however, the Spirit of God enabled him to talk with great boldness. Those present noted that, as he spoke, such was his fervour and joy that his feet moved as if in dancing, and that he seemed to glow with the fire of divine love.[35]

In the 2010 series of Big Brother, one of the contestants, Dave Vaughan, entered the house wearing a monk's habit. The "Happy Monk", as he came to be known, was often heard telling the other housemates "It's all in the glory!" and that's what the crowd were shouting when he left the house as runner-up 13 weeks later. In a follow up interview for a Christian radio station, Cross Rhythms, he explained what the phrase meant: "For the last four to five years my life has been one of really encountering God's manifest presence ... That presence I like to call the glory. It's also the beauty and the goodness of the Lord ... It's the manifest, tangible presence of the Lord ... that we carry on a daily basis. I just love the glory, I just love seeing God move and touch people."[36]

There's something in each of us that seeks to experience, in one way or another, the reality of God in our lives. When I look back on my life I can identify a variety of occasions when I've suddenly found myself up close and personal with the Creator of the Universe! There was the service that I attended as a questioning unbeliever, when having told God I couldn't work him out, and that he would have to show me if he were real, he did just that! Somehow in a church full of people, all I was aware of was me, the preacher and God. Then there was the time I was stuck on the top of a glacier with my American friend, Jeff, who had just badly gashed his leg on a rock. We were in the middle of nowhere, hadn't seen anybody all day, and had barely enough time to get back to the campsite before sunset. Straight after sending a desperate prayer skywards three men appeared over the glacial ridge and one of them, a doctor with a first aid kit, dressed the wound and sent us on our way.

Maybe you've had similar incidents – times when, at least for a moment, you *know* that God exists. But it's not just in conversion experiences or dramatic answers to prayer that we are aware of God's glory. As a good Baptist, I'm a little hesitant to admit that one of the times God revealed himself to me was in an Augustinian Priory as I prayed silently at the shrine of the Mother of Good Counsel. Perhaps more embarrassingly, God even met me when, slightly reluctantly, I agreed to be a participant in a Christian dance workshop! We are all different, and while some will sense God's presence in a simple act of kindness, others will be moved by God's

119

wisdom in a particular verse of Scripture, or stirred by the singing of a rousing hymn.

Such occurrences are rarely predictable, and they cannot be manufactured, but we can, as God's people, choose to live in the desire and expectancy of his glory being made manifest. The Baptist Union, in describing their fifth core value, affirm that churches are called to be "worshipping" communities and quote Sister Margaret Magdalen who says: "Deep is the joy ... of those who hunger and thirst for God, his righteousness and his kingdom, with the intensity and all consuming desire of desert dwellers in drought."[37] We worship God when our deepest longing is to know God and to see his will being fulfilled in and through us; and it is in this act of glorifying God that we are able to experience the joy of being in his presence.

Jesus tells us that all who seek God will find him[38] – and as they find him they are changed by him. Scripture tells us again and again that an encounter with the glory of God transforms lives in a real and tangible way. Take, for example, the story of Moses who, returning from his second trip to the top of Mount Sinai, spoke to the people of Israel and "His face was radiant because he had spoken with the LORD." (Exodus 34:29) It seems he literally glowed as a result of having spent so long in the glory, and I don't know about you, but in my life I've met a few people who also seemed to have exuded God. These people don't even need to say anything – somehow just by looking at them you know that they've recently been in the presence of God.

In some ways I guess it's a bit like being in love – there's always something about the glint in the eye or in the lightness of spirit which gives the game away. When Christ has won our hearts, people will notice that it's hard to stop gazing in his direction, and perhaps that's why the psalmist tells us that: "Those who look to him are radiant." (Psalm 34:5) It's interesting too that in Ephesians, as Paul talks about mutual submission within marriage, he uses the same word "radiant" (Ephesians 5:17) to describe the church which has been transformed by the self-giving love of Christ.

So often when we gather together as church we seem to be more concerned about the externals of what we do – for example, whether we're singing ancient hymns or modern songs – than about the internal attitude of our hearts. The glory of God can be witnessed in the highest of Anglican liturgies and in the wildest of Pentecostal assemblies; what makes the difference to how people leave, is how they come. This doesn't mean that we can forget about making what we do culturally relevant to the people we are trying to reach – but it does mean that whatever we do, when God's people are already captivated by him, then it's more likely that others will be too.

When God's big-heart envelops us, as individuals and as churches, and we come to know the full extent of his love for us, and for the world he has made, we will more and more become the radiant or "glory-glowing" churches that he has created us to be. But it can't just be when we gather together that we should hope to experience the glory of God – we can't be waiting until the weekend for our spiritual fix to help get us through the week as the glow won't last that long! We need to nurture a desire and an expectancy of God-encounters every minute of every day, and seek to know God's will for each aspect of our lives. How can I glorify God in my family, in my friendships, in my leisure time, and through my work?

Cast your minds back to the couple I mentioned in my introduction, sat in the café searching for that elusive something in the pages of a magazine and through the connections of a social network. It is possible that God has already started revealing himself to them – many people outside church will tell you of their own spiritual experiences. What may well be missing from their lives, however, is the gospel narrative which explains how, through Jesus, the living God longs to embrace them with his love. But if I do decide to go across to them and introduce them to Christ, what is it that will make the difference? Whilst it's helpful to memorise Bible verses, and evangelistic tools have their place, what really matters will be whether, in some small way, by his Spirit, I am reflecting the glory of God. If my whole life is an act of worship, then I don't have to wait for them to come to church next Sunday to encounter Jesus, maybe they will be able to meet him, in me, here in this café.

Indeed as I reflect upon these last five chapters, I'm a bit reluctant to invite them to my church anyway. We're not as gospel telling, gospel dwelling, generously giving, grace growing or glory glowing as we should be – and they might be disappointed! Thankfully, God's big-heart is so full of mercy, that when we humbly turn to him in our weakness, he comes in his power[39] and transforms our imperfect churches into communities that really can change the world.

Big-Hearted Beginners – Part 5

In a desire to be mission focused, relevant and accessible, it can be easy to lose sight of the fact that it is only through an encounter with the living God that lives are transformed. At RE:NEW we are conscious of the need for people to be meeting with him on a daily basis, as well as when we are gathering together. We are also aware of the diverse ways in which different individuals experience the presence of God.

Although we no longer use the Lode Chapel for our Sunday morning services, its peaceful rural location means that it is well suited as a venue for retreats and prayerful reflection. Through working in partnership with a local Baptist minister who has a ministry of spiritual direction, we now offer regular quiet days for the benefit of the RE:NEW and wider church community. The chapel is also the venue for a monthly contemplative service, called "Sacred Space", where people find that they are able to meet with God in the silence.

Whether we are singing loud contemporary songs in the school hall or traditional hymns in a service at the local care home; whether we are watching a DVD and discussing it over a cup of coffee in the RE:NEW Café or studying the Bible at home or in one of our small groups; whether we are doing the actions to a song in the Kids Club praise party or serving the community in some way or another; in all of these activities our intention is to worship him and bring glory to his name.

BIG
HEARTED

SECTION 3

Big-Hearted Evangelism

Two piles of two kinds of stuff

If you and I could make two piles of two kinds of stuff,
One that measured the go and the other labelled theory
or talking about it you know, that kind of guff,
The go and do would be dwarfed by the other,
The command to go suffocated by the clever theory
smother,
As if we follow a loser who gave a great, grand
suggestion, good intention, that wasn't really news.
Enough of the excuses of not being my thing or cup of tea
or, thank you, on this matter I have my own views,
The command you see is to go.
Yeah I know,
Yet it's ok to say no, no
To the urgent majestic decree I am slow,
Even though the King aches so so so
Much for everyone we are called to go, go, go.
(A poem by Chris Duffett)

Writing about serving a Big-Hearted God and living out being a Big-Hearted Church is all very well and good, but what can we actually do to play our part in reaching those around us with the good news of Jesus? How can each one of us put into practice what we have just read?

You see, as Christians we are so good at talking about mission and how to reach people, but we don't do so well in implementing our good intentions. For all the fine talk, clever methodologies, mission statements and sentiments, there is a travesty of an imbalance between this and the face-to-face good news sharing that happens. Don't get me wrong: groups of Christians up and down the country are sharing and showing the good news, but we need to do so much more.

Therefore, without apology, this section is soaked with principles that have a practical dynamic to them. Please don't think I'm stipulating how big-hearted evangelism has to be done. My teaching comes from a simple ministry: 1) I love people; and 2) I use the abilities God has given me to engage with them. I'm not itching to present a new formula or a new name for letting others in on what it means to be a Christian. You will be gifted differently to me and undoubtedly made able to do things by God in ways that I could never dream of doing. Between us all, there are so many ways we can reach out to our friends and family and even strangers in our communities; the key is actually to take action and commit to changing this world through the good news.

In my travels and when I have opportunities to teach, I often meet eager groups of Christians who ask me what they can do to reach out into their communities. At times it seems as if they want to have a formula or some kind of evangel-

enchantment potion so that they will be able to share the good news of Jesus with confidence, have a good time doing it, and those who they engage with will have a good time too. The advice I give to them is what I pass on to you: do something! This may not sound particularly spiritual to you, yet actually engaging with people to let them know what you believe is profoundly spiritual. That's where the magic happens. Remember, when we go to *do something*, Jesus teaches us that this is in partnership with God who is wonderfully involved in all aspects of our communities and is himself longing for the people of the world. This *going* to reach people and teach others what you have as a Christian is his idea. The simple act of going to show the good news of Jesus means we meet with God in doing it. I appreciate the promise Jesus gives his friends which also applies to us today when we intentionally take action to let others know the good news: "...I am with you." (Matthew 28:20) However, I do have some Christian friends who still believe that doing evangelism is somehow unnecessary, that it is in some way strangely removed from God and that going to do something is one way or another usurping what God really wants to do. This kind of thinking is bizarre to me; I believe our Father aches for the hurting and lost. I imagine him holding his breath in anticipation for multitudes to return and find their home in the lives that they were always created to have, in relationship with him through Jesus. So, in reaching out to others in this world we experience something of what God cares about and we also get to share his heart with those who don't know him as we do. Every moment, every person, every conversation is an opportunity for the living Christ to breathe through you, reach out through you and touch the lives of those around you. He longs to embrace people using your arms.

Sheila is one of my volunteer city centre chaplains. She loves offering free hugs. She happily stands in a busy street with a sign declaring "Free Hug". She waits. I have seen, time and time again, people touched by God through this simple gesture. One man received peace through having one of Sheila's special hugs and felt he could confide in her about a burden he had been carrying for years. He wept as the guilt rolled away and he confessed to a hugging complete stranger what had gone on in his life. Sheila was willing to show the love of God and be there to listen.

God uses this simple gesture of Sheila's. It's unsophisticated, yet an example of *going*. It expresses acceptance and speaks of the one who came to embrace the poor, lonely and outcast. One woman recently turned up especially for one of Sheila's special hugs. Why? She had received one the previous week. That one was her first hug in two years. That's no lie. She hadn't been embraced in all that time and on finding a lady willing to hug her, the chance to come back for a second one was too good to be true.

Being willing to *go* and do something is vital for two reasons. Firstly, for the welfare and quality of life for the people around us: people need Jesus. Secondly, when we actually engage in gospel sharing, it renews us. As we go, we rely on one another and the Holy Spirit. We learn new things, receive new gifts and encounter Christ in others.

I hope by now you have read enough of this book to catch some inspiration so that you may be geared up to go and do something. At this point I reckon it will be useful to give you two indicators which you may experience as you prepare to do something big-hearted, especially if this kind of going to do something is new to you. When I'm preparing to go and speak to people or to show something of what I believe, I must admit that what I often experience is the sense of being terrified! I prepare to step out and do something new and I feel rather foolish. Yet it seems to be in those places of weakness that God empowers me and gives me strength and things happen around me which I just can't explain. Often *peace* is one of the indicators that church leaders say we need if we are working out how to do God's will. I actually think it's the opposite. It's when my heart is beating like a drum, my palms are sweaty and I nervously step out and do something to bring the good news of Jesus to people that I see God at work around me. Don't get me wrong, I'm not suggesting it's all down to me and my terrifying encounters, there is however, a definite partnership that occurs when we *go*. This panicked nervousness happens on quite a regular basis as I offer to pray for people on the streets.

Let me give you an example of apprehensively reaching out to people in the name of Jesus. I led a team in the popular evangelism foray of *Treasure Hunting*, which gives a useful structure and focus for bringing what is on God's heart to people around us. If you haven't come across it before, it is a simple tool to use where small teams work together and ask God for clues under five different headings. They then venture out wherever the clues take them: shops, parks or even up to people's homes! In short, it's using revelatory phenomena in evangelism. Or as my friend, Aliss Cresswell, says: "The Holy Sprit tells you something about someone that you couldn't naturally know."[40] Here's a confession: I find Treasure Hunting very difficult to do, yet I believe in prophetic evangelism! So, I'm often scared stiff when leading teams learning how to do it.

Here's the example of one of my daunting experiences. One summer I led teams of people out into the streets of St Andrews so that some brave souls in New Wine Scotland could put into practice, out and about on the streets, the teaching they were receiving in seminars. After giving a briefing about what we were going to do, we were to write down the clues we believed God was giving us. Nervously I joined a small team and, on the top of my list, for some strange reason, I found myself writing the word "crocodile"! In my prayer needs section, among some other clues, I wrote "left shoulder pain". As I left to go and meet the people whom we hoped might be our treasure, I shook my head at my clues, unsure why I felt God had given me "crocodile" as one of them.

An hour later our treasure hunt is over and I'm somewhat dazed and in shock. It is with a certain sense of unbelief that I debrief the team while holding a stone model crocodile given to me as a memento by the man with the painful left shoulder who asked me to pray for him. He was chuffed that he had turned out to be our treasure and was grateful that we would pray for his shoulder too. This crocodile made me realise that even though I was nervous, heart pounding and feeling out of my depth, God uses these moments. If we wait for our hearts to be *full of peace* we simply won't do much; instead our hearts need to be stretched as we do new things.

The second feeling we may have as we prepare for engaging in more big-hearted evangelism is love for people. This can be a useful balance to the racing heart and sticky palms of being absolutely terrified! The question that holds all this teaching together is this: Do you love people? You see, without love for others it is very difficult to engage in big-hearted evangelism. Like my friend Sheila, I also enjoy hugging people and often stand in city centres looking like a right idiot with my well used worn sign. But if it was all about the hugs and nothing to do with my concern for people around me then I would have to stop. You see, the day I cease caring for those around me is the day I believe I need to evaluate the motives of why I do what I do. This also applies to my attitude towards those I have known for some time and who have become friends. To help me keep a check on this when I meet up with friends or arrange evenings down the local pub I sometimes give myself a bit of a quick Motive MOT:

> "Do I love my friends because I want them to become Christians or do I want them to become Christians because I love them?"

This love that we have for others helps us see God in them and be willing to affirm the unique way they have been made.

Big-hearted evangelism sees God in others

When the Spirit of God invades you there's a consequence that you don't anticipate. It's this: that you find yourself very sensitive to Jesus' suffering in other people. People become sacramental. That's what St. Francis of Assisi tried to tell us. People are viewed as kind of vehicles through whom Jesus comes to us, so that when we look into their eyes we have this eerie awareness that Jesus is staring back at us. That's what it means to be a Christian, to be filled with God and to be sensitive to Jesus, waiting to be loved in needy people"[41] Tony Campolo

We need to get over the notion that people who are not Christians are separated from God. This just isn't Biblical. You see, while people may be separated from God by their sin, God cannot be separated to them by their sin. See the difference? In my book, *Smack Heads and Fat Cats,* I argue that even the originals of all mess-ups, Adam and Eve, were engaged with and communicated with God. Even though their fall is the inheritance of every human being ever born, God patiently measures them up for some clothes and sits with them as he makes them.

People who do not know God are still made in his image. God still remains their Father even if they are unaware of that and I believe he wants, to the point of aching, for them to become children of his. Even though people may have yet to come to the knowledge of the truth, when we spend time with them we are still able to see God in them, working in them, teaching them, looking after them and gently guiding them back home.

Last week I bought two croissants for breakfast as I had an early morning train journey and thought they would go handsomely with my coffee. I then had an awful thought: perhaps one of them was meant for someone else? I hoped not. They just looked too good and buttery. I sat at a table for two on the train and just before the train left a young man, who had rushed on, sat opposite me. I felt that the first thing I needed to say was: "Would you like one of these croissants? They're really good." It was as if I had pre-arranged a two hour breakfast meeting to discuss Jesus with this young man. He had question after question about my faith and I wanted to hear what he believed too. I learnt so much from him and I hope he learnt something too. I shared with him some of the things I saw that God had gifted him with: leadership gifts as well as wisdom. The guy seemed to be quite moved by the way I recognised something of his heart and the gifting within him. The sacrificing of one of the croissants was worth it. This kind of affirming experience also happened to me on Palm Sunday when I felt inspired to do something slightly out of the ordinary. Okay, truthfully, it was really quite odd! I set up a stall in the city centre with a big sign that declared: "Free Palm Cross Reading". The idea was to offer a Palm Cross on which I would write some words of knowledge for people and read to them what I believed was on God's heart for them. The hope was that I would be able to communicate something that would strengthen, comfort and encourage. (1 Corinthians 14:3) A colleague joined me in this venture and he made a stall next to mine, where people could fill small plastic Easter egg shells with chocolates and a message of hope. We agreed that if three or four people were to come to my stall throughout the morning, then it would be well worth the effort. I ended up having a queue.

During the Sunday morning around 40 people came and sat opposite me and asked for a Palm Cross Reading. A woman, who was dressed ever so smartly and looked very business-like, sat opposite me. I felt God say that she was like a farmer and was good at making things grow. I also felt him say that he would protect her home. Afterwards she thanked me and went to speak to her husband, a big tattooed burly bloke who was standing by my colleague's Easter egg stall. She told him to go and queue up and have "one done". He was reluctant, but she insisted and then showed him what I had written on the Palm Cross. "Look at this! I didn't tell him anything about me and he wrote this!" she declared. So, he grudgingly obeyed his wife and went and joined the short queue. When he sat down to have his Palm Cross, the first thing he said was: "I suppose you are going to write how I am going to go to hell." I gently said, "No, I'm going to write how much God loves you and the ways he has gifted you and made you." Then I did. I don't remember what qualities I wrote about him on that small Palm cross, but I do remember the guy's reaction. He simply sat there and cried.

Recognising people's God-given gifts, even if they don't believe in God, is a wonderful way of showing our faith in a generous way. When we do it, we lift people up who so desperately need affirming. Yes, our observations may be misunderstood, yet may I encourage you as you meet with people simply to say what you see as their gifts in their lives and to wait and see what their reaction is. I guarantee you will have some priceless moments. In his book *Celebrity Culture*, John Drane argues the need for Christians to show a sense of the worth and value of people. Why? - "... because we are widely perceived as judgemental, quick to speak in condemnation of others but having little else to say."[42]

On a number of occasions, I have noticed people when I have been on trains or in the street and I have thought what amazing pastors they would make. So (with my heart thumping and feeling terrified) I tell them. Yes, I must admit there have been awkward moments where I have had to explain what I meant, but one guy was so touched by the gesture he shook my hand and thanked me for recognising that in him. One of our lovely neighbours often calls round with gifts of pies and has quite a gift of making the rounds and calling on elderly or lonely people in our village. "You're like a vicar!" I tell him.

Having this kind of attitude in our encounters with our friends and with people whom we may randomly meet is also a great blessing to us. I enjoy meeting ardent militant atheists. I used to get somewhat flustered by them, but now my encounters are rather enjoyable, not because I like to argue or discuss different theories of God's existence or not, but because I'm often pleasantly distracted as I can't help thinking how clever they are. I listen to their arguments and the way they think and how they have been made by God and I marvel. The irony, of course, is that God should create people with such intellectual brilliance that for some it turns them away from their very creator and makes them a bit smug. I must admit that on these occasions I do have a certain degree of satisfaction telling atheists how clever I think they are and how God has made them with such brilliant minds.

Recently I was asked to pray for a little Muslim boy who couldn't speak. I say asked, but actually I was more coerced, when the boy pointed from his wheelchair and using sign language absolutely insisted that I pray. His father asked: "Do you want a special prayer for healing?" The boy nodded and pointed to my hand and then to his head. I knelt next to him and prayed that Jesus would enable him to speak and I commanded in Jesus' name for him to be made well. I also thanked God for what I saw in this boy's life, such trust and peace. The presence of God fell upon us and I can't explain it other than to say that God's company was delightfully right there on the street. The little Muslim boy beamed with joy and his face seemed to shine. I explained to the father of the boy that there was so much joy around us and that his son had an incredible gift of joy. He agreed. One of my chaplain volunteers, David, said it was like seeing a modern day retelling of the story where Moses' face shone when he met with God. How would you have felt if a Muslim dad and son had asked you to pray for them? I simply recognised God working in their lives and affirmed what I saw.

The most thrilling example of a Jesus follower recognising God in others is from the story found in Acts 10. It is the story of the birth of the Gentile Church. Peter is a guest at a friend's house and while he is waiting for dinner to be prepared he is on the top of the house on a flat roof, a kind of balcony type patio area. While he is there he has a vision of a white sheet lowered down before his eyes containing all kinds of unclean foods, which as a Jew he isn't allowed to touch or eat. He is commanded three times to get up and kill and then tuck into what he sees before him. Peter insists that he has never eaten anything impure or unclean and refuses to do so, three times. As Peter argues his case for not touching or eating anything he shouldn't, a voice announces: "Do not call anything impure that God has made clean." (Acts 10:15) While Peter is contemplating the vision, the Spirit of God says to Peter: "Simon, three men are looking for you. So get up and go downstairs. Do not hesitate to go with them, for I have sent them."[43] (Acts 10:20) The men Peter is confronted with are Gentiles, the very kind of people he had grown up avoiding. These were the people who were excluded from God's plan of salvation, because they weren't Jewish. Here Peter is confronted by God, who is saying "go" with these men! Peter ends up travelling back to their master's home, a man who is called Cornelius. Meanwhile, Cornelius has also been having his own communication with God, just as Peter has, yet he isn't a Christian! Acts 10 describes him as devout and God fearing, someone who gave generously to those in need and who also prayed regularly. In the story, just before we are told about Peter's vision of the unclean foods, Cornelius has an encounter with an angel. This angel declares: "Your prayers and neighbourly acts have brought you to God's attention." (Acts 10:4 The Message) It is in the context of all this heavenly communication that Peter arrives to find that Cornelius has gathered all his family and friends and crammed them into his living room to hear what Peter has to say. Does Peter recognise God in them and the situation as something God has been working in? Does Peter see how God has moved in the hearts of these people? Yes, and he is given a huge lesson as he goes; it is a moment that changes his life forever and, thankfully, changes ours too. You see, without this story of the birth of the Gentile Church, those of us who are not Jewish would have remained excluded by the beliefs of the first Christians, who thought Jesus was only given for the lost sheep of Israel. I'm so pleased that Peter declared back then: "Now I am certain that God treats all people alike. (Acts 10:34) He then delivers a message of good news of peace in Jesus Christ. As he speaks the Holy Spirit falls upon them and they start speaking in new tongues and prophesying! This is glorious!

Peter had to recognise God in these people. He didn't exclude them by his rules and ways of understanding what it means to be a Christian. One holiday, Seth, my son, and I, checked out a Greek Orthodox service, on the advice of fellow Light Project evangelist, Glyn Jones. He said: "It's an experience!" So with his commendation of a right ol' adventure off we tootled on the bus down to the main little town of the small Greek island; my wife and the girls chickened out and stayed at home with a leisurely breakfast.

The first thing we encountered was that the packed bus was full of churchgoers in their finest garb. There were people we recognised from the beach and local shopkeepers, as well as the elderly couple who had made me an island hero sensation by telling everyone that I had saved their lives by rescuing them from drowning, when the truth was I had simply given them a hand up when a wave knocked them over on the shore!

We followed the crowd and to our amazement the service had already started. Chanting was drifting through the open windows of the brilliant-white building and people were overflowing through the doors. It seemed to be a bit of a scramble to get in, so we pushed and squeezed into the throng with the sound of the chatting congregation and the chanting of the heavily bearded priest in our ears. Seth said: "Dad, why are we here? This is a different religion, isn't it?" I chuckled and tried to explain the differences and what people were doing, but to be honest I didn't quite get what was going on, so I looked confident and followed the crowds towards the front of a huge altar on which were golden images and an amazingly beautiful ornate golden cross. It was an awesome sight.

The chanting continued and we watched people around us kiss images and pictures of different scenes; some I recognised from the Bible, and others I didn't. Seth and I gave quizzical looks to each other. He squeezed my hand and said: "Dad, what are they doing?" I explained that I thought we should follow everyone to the guy at the front who was giving people something out of a big cup. All around us, people had big rock-sized chunks of bread in their hands, and hungry children were chomping away on them.

We finally got to the guy at the front, who I then worked out was most definitely the priest. He had a long beard and tall hat, his clothing immaculate; his cassock was overlaid with even more golden garments. The woman in front of me spoke to me and pointed to the red cloth in the priest's hands which was underneath an old golden cup that he was also holding. I asked: "What do I do?" The Priest looked me straight in the eye and shouted: "Greek Orthodox?" I was rather flustered and Seth grabbed my arm and jumped as the

Priest shouted. I said, "Um, no." "Greek Orthodox?" he sternly asked again. "I am a Christian," I declared. The Priest then said equally as strongly as before, while shielding the cup with his hand as if I were just about to dip my finger in, "ONLY Greek Orthodox!" I stood before him for a few painful seconds and said in an Englishman on holiday come Oliver Twist type of way: "What should I do?" He pointed to a big basket containing the chunky bits of bread. We went over and Seth happily grabbed some out of the huge basket. I politely took a chunk, but it felt heavy in my hands and the thought crossed my mind that, come the most convenient time, I would hurl it away in protest. I walked down from the beautiful front of the church feeling left out, a follower of Christ barred from communion.

After I had calmed down and we had observed the service some more, I weighed up the experience while humbly chewing on my bread taken from the basket for those who are not in the know or *in*. It tasted good. Even though we may be from a tradition a million-miles away from the structures and exclusivity of Greek Orthodoxy and we may have an informality and non-conformity to our services, we can still find ourselves trapped within the traditions and rituals which exclude those who may seek to enter in and taste what we have to offer.

Who is it that we may know or randomly meet who we need to see what God is doing in their lives? How can we welcome them into our church family?

Big-Hearted evangelism seeks to do the works of Jesus

Yet, how will the sacred scarred healing hands reach out to those who are bereft of Messiah comfort unless Saints meet, Face to face with the public, in public in the parks, shops or street?
Taken from "Saints on the Street", a poem I wrote sat in ASDA café on a Sunday morning

In the early Church, evangelism was done in the particular context of people being passionate about Jesus and what he had done. In Acts chapter 4 there is a short story of Peter and John and how others observed them. People saw: 1) their courage; 2) that they were unschooled, ordinary men; and 3) that they had been with Jesus. It wasn't that long since they had been spending time with him and seen him alive after witnessing his horrific death. Like those commanded in Bible times to *go*, we also need a passion that comes from having been with Jesus. *Going* without the closeness of Jesus can lead to a shallow kind of evangelism, one that is empty of love for people and one that is bereft of being rooted into Jesus and his power. There are no short cuts if we seek to do the works of Jesus, as this will mean being close to him in a position where the Holy Spirit may flow through us for others to enjoy tangibly, and not just theoretically. This kind of closeness changes evangelism from a *have to* to a *love to* kind of experience.

The book of Acts is full of the examples of the first friends of Jesus doing his works, which resulted in people around them being filled with wonder and amazement through the signs and wonders that were performed. People were even raised from the dead, like the lady called Dorcas, who was prayed for by Peter. She was known for doing "good and helping the poor" and after being prepared for burial was brought back to life! (Acts 9:36-41) I long to see, with my own eyes, works of Jesus like this.

One summer, before leading some street outreach in Glasgow city centre, I took some of my team out for a bite to eat. We grabbed some spicy noodles and, with my lips still burning and eyes still watering from a healthy portion of chilli eating bravado, we hurried back to meet up with the rest of the team at a local hotel. As we crossed the road, one of the team members saw a lady hobbling along on crutches, with her daughter walking alongside her. He bounded up to her like some kind of evangelical Tigger and asked what was wrong, in the same breath saying that, if she liked, he would pray for her! A somewhat brazen approach, I must admit. It seemed as though no one had offered to pray for her before and the lady said: "Okay, I've got nothing to lose." We found out soon afterwards why she thought this, as she was booked in to have an operation to have her leg amputated in two weeks' time and *really* didn't have anything to lose by agreeing to be prayed for.

After a few seconds of prayer, the lady began to cry. When my friend asked what was the matter, she explained that she had felt his hands on her foot. This may not sound particularly extraordinary to you. It didn't to us either, until the lady explained that she hadn't had any feeling in her leg or foot for over four years. Her daughter was astounded and phoned other family members on her mobile and started explaining what was happening. As we stood outside MacDonald's, people started gathering around us to see what the commotion was about. The lady was amazed. Some of the team gently shared about the love of God with her.

I'm not sure what happened to that lady, whether in the end she needed her leg amputated or not. But as someone who witnessed what happened just by standing on the edge of the circle of the hubbub, I was blown away by the impact a simple prayer had on this lady's life. It was a great reminder that as Christians we are commissioned to do some freaky stuff. Jesus declares we will place our hands on sick people and they will get well. (Mark 16:18) This lavish big-hearted approach that my friend was happy to have a go at challenged me to be more up-front with people about the healing power of Jesus. You see, Jesus declared to his first friends that they would do the same works that he had done and indeed greater works than he had done, because he was going to the Father. (John 14:12)

Are you willing to ask people if you may pray for them? When you do, you might just observe Jesus by his Spirit reach out and touch people's lives in front of your eyes. This phenomenon may be within the safe confines of a church building, but, more often than not, my experience is that miracles happen *out there*. It's in this partnership with Jesus as we seek to emulate his works of healing that something can happen which is way beyond our own resources and we see his power at work.

When my daughter Beatrice was a toddler she used to enjoy pulling me around the shallow swimming pool by my toes, as I laid on my back. The water somehow made it easy to guide my rather ample bulk over the shallow pool with some gentle pulling from small hands which seemingly became superhuman and strong in the water. Back on dry land it's a very different story. When we are willing to have a go at doing something seemingly impossible it will take us by surprise what will happen. I have been shocked when I have ventured into places where I least expect God to act. I experience the unmistakable tangible presence of Holy God in squats sharing a meal with people who are homeless, in drug dens praying as people prepare to shoot up, in Alcoholics Anonymous meetings, in prisons, in young offender institutions, sitting on a pavement with someone begging, in psychiatric wards holding the hand of a drugged-up suicidal young person, in law courts, in office buildings, at car boot sales, at football matches and at the side of freshly dug graves during the funerals of young men whose lives have been tragically cut short. These are the places I have experienced the unmistakable tangible presence of the one who loves to go and be amongst broken, bruised and battered people, and as I've prayed, people have been healed. I can't really explain why or how. It's just that Jesus seems to do what he does in the places we would least expect, for people who we may think are somehow unredeemable as their lives are so messed up.

For me, I have experienced his presence at church services too, but recently I experienced Jesus while tucking into a bowl of macaroni cheese. It literally felt as if the Holy Spirit fell on me. Admittedly, I was being prayed for at the time as I munched on my dinner at the kitchen table. My children kept looking at my left eye, which was swollen up and had red bits where there should have been white bits; it was oozing a bit too. To be honest they were a bit grossed out by it. My son, Seth, put down his fork and, with his mouth full of macaroni cheese, stretched out his hand and prayed: "Right Jesus, just as you healed people and they were completely made better, I ask in your name for you to heal my dad right now." I said thanks to Seth and thought what a kind thing it was that he should pray for me, when, unexpectedly and as I carried on eating, I had the most amazing sensation rush through my body. For a few minutes, it felt as if someone's hands were upon, around, and, rather strangely, *in* my head. Soon afterwards, my eye was completely better, much to the amusement of my three children.

Seeking to do the work of Jesus doesn't just mean the exhilarating healing that we can share in with him. Doing the work of Jesus also means the costly choice of being incarnational. The story of Warren Park Cafe Church told by Barney Barron shows what I mean by this:

"My family and I moved from an affluent Hampshire village to a large housing estate, considered to be an area of high deprivation. We moved with the intention of church planting on the estate, with a passion to reach the unchurched.

We soon became aware that others had tried and failed to church plant in the area, therefore there was only a small and struggling Anglo-Catholic church in existence on the estate. Previous attempts to church plant included a 'new church' network who rented a school hall on Sunday, put on a charismatic worship event and invited people to join them. No one from the church was prepared to live on the estate, because of its poor housing and bad reputation. They were disappointed that no one joined their church service and retreated back to the mother church.

Another attempt was by a similar 'new church' network. This group did have a number of members move on to the estate. In addition to hiring a local hall for Sunday morning worship, they put on other evangelistic events. This included tent missions and a weekly kids club. Although the kids club did attract large numbers of children, they failed to engage with the community beyond that and again retreated back to the mother church.

I had moved to the estate with a traditional model of church planting in mind, but quickly realised these 'attractional,' 'come to us', models of evangelism were not going to work. I also realised how far removed my own middle class cultural background was from the culture of the estate. I had a lot to learn about my own understanding of God, Church and what exactly the 'good news' is for the people of this estate.

My family and I chose an incarnational rather than attractional approach to mission. For two years we didn't organise any meetings or put on any events. Instead we became immersed in the local community. Our children go to the local schools, and have joined local clubs. My wife and I became school governors, joined the residents' committee and got involved with the local children's centre. We also spent time making friends with local people and having fun! Just as God stepped into human skin in the person of Jesus, we became fully immersed members of this community. They are our friends not merely 'souls to win for Jesus'. We have built trust with local people meaning people will ask us about our faith and seek after God without a need for us to preach.

We have also won the trust of other agencies being given more opportunities than we could ever deliver. Currently, I run a weekly dads' club for the local children's centre, and my wife runs a listening service one afternoon in the same centre. A group of us run Solace, a listening service in the local secondary school and we have formed a partnership with a local youth counselling service. The Youth Service asked us to run their front line youth work, as due to government cuts they are no longer able to deliver this. That means we get the use of their resources and facilities for free.

We do also run some of our own activities including a family fun time, a faith and football league and a holiday club. Our main gathering is cafe church which meets in the children's centre on Friday evening. Cafe Church has all the ingredients of church as you may know it, worship, discipleship, community, and mission, just in a format you might not recognise at first, aims to be reflective of the community that we are in, rather than the middle class, Christendom culture that I have grown up in.

We haven't experienced revival yet. However we have seen a steady stream of new believers being baptised each year. We have also seen a change in the community in various ways. The primary school and the secondary school had recently been in special measures when we moved to the estate. Both schools this year received outstanding Ofsteds and the secondary school was first in the country for contextual value added. There seems to be greater community cohesion and people feeling empowered to make a difference in their community. I am not claiming this is all down to us, but we should expect to see transformation when the people of God move into a community and pray for his kingdom to come and his will be done in that place and become agents of that change.

What I have learnt through this experience is that if we want to stem the decline of the church, we need to stop worrying about the church and engage with the world outside. Most people in this current generation have never been to church so expecting them to come to our Sunday morning services, or even an evangelistic event is increasingly futile. Standing on the street corner banging the gospel drum, door to door visitation and many of our traditional evangelistic methods are largely ineffective in an age where Christians are increasingly marginalised. There is no shortcut to engaging with our communities. If we are open to learn from people beyond the bounds of church, we may just grow in our understanding of God as we enter a new journey of discovery in the communities in which we live and work."

Barney and his family's approach to doing the works of Jesus speaks of how much value they place on others. This attitude follows in Jesus' footsteps, as he had an uncanny knack of presenting how much he thought people were worth in the most outrageous ways. He often shared this symbolically through stories and parables, such as the lost sheep where the farmer leaves a flock of 99 to search for the precious lost one, or the lost son who is given half his inheritance early and, when that is all squandered, is lavishly welcomed home and receives even more.

He also taught us how much he valued people through the stories that have been recorded of things he did, like the one about the crazy man in the tombs who cut himself with rocks and couldn't be chained up. This man has a "legion" of demons in him and when Jesus turns up they don't waste any time in pleading with him that, if he makes them leave the man, he'll let them possess the herd of pigs up on the hillside instead. Now pigs aren't cheap! According to an online web site for wannabe smallholders, a pig costs £225 to buy and raise ready for the butcher. In the story of Jesus' encounter with the man there were quite a number of pigs; in fact Mark, who recorded the story, reckoned there were "about two thousand" of them. (Mark 5:13) So, let's just get our head round this with some modern day cash: £450,000 worth of pigs were given to a legion of demons to possess with the result that they all ran into the sea and were washed away. All this happened for the sake of freedom for one man. The gospels don't record much about the reaction of the farmers, other than they pleaded with Jesus to leave their region. (Mark 5:17) The Message paraphrase puts it like this: "At first they were in awe — and then they were upset, upset over the drowned pigs. They demanded that Jesus leave and not come back." I'm not surprised they were upset; what a waste of money over one crazy man whom Jesus thought fit to make free and "in his right mind". Jesus placed the cost of that one man's freedom at nearly half a million pounds.

I'm not sure who ended up paying for the lost herd of pigs; I suspect the farmers footed the bill. There is something in that story that makes me think that Jesus was willing to use other people's possessions for the sake of the health and well-being of a tortured oppressed man. I wonder: could this story challenge how much money we are willing to use on maintenance of what we do as church rather than on mission?

Another eye-wateringly expensive story is the one of the woman who anoints Jesus using an alabaster jar of perfume. She cracks it open and, according to Luke's account, she pours the perfume on his feet. Mark describes the same story, but has her anointing Jesus' head. Jesus got covered! This lavish perfume pouring, pre-embalming, got people quite upset, not least the disciples who thought it a waste of perfume: "It could have been sold for more than a year's wages and the money given to the poor. And they rebuked her harshly." (Mark 14:5) Currently, the average wage of someone living in the UK is around £27,500. So let's imagine this was the cost of the perfume. No wonder Jesus announces that she has done a good thing for him! He must have smelt amazing! What does this story teach us? Jesus didn't seem to struggle with exuberance for the sake of the gospel, either in rescuing someone or in showing devotion to him.

I used a small amount of money recently to show generosity. It wasn't much; it was fifty pounds that someone had given to me to invest in the work that I do. So, after pondering what to do, I gave it to Greggs the Bakers on a Sunday morning. I popped into the local shop and simply presented them with an unusual request: May I give you some money on behalf of the church in Peterborough to pay for your customers' breakfast or brunch or whatever? It turned out that they hadn't had such a request before, so the area manager needed to be consulted.

Ten minutes later they confirm that my unusual request would be *nice*. While the staff in Greggs are offering food for free, a small team of us give out some free hugs on the streets. There is a lot of puzzlement about why we are offering hugs and why free breakfast is on offer. Soon people want to talk and thank us for cheering up their day! The ladies working in Greggs do a great job as newly inducted evangelists. "Would you like the church to pay for this for you?" I hear the assistant manager ask as one after another people come to pay. At the end of the morning, one of the ladies working in

Greggs explains to me what it is like to offer their goods for free: "It was a lovely thing to do, most people were shocked!"

Jesus' exuberant approach to people wasn't just about the price of pigs or receiving expensive perfume. He was able to notice the people around him and treat them as valuable. This is the biggest challenge for me in some of the work I do as a city centre chaplain. There isn't any set routine or patter for the work I do, it is simply a case of looking around and seeing people, taking the opportunities to listen and help when they arise.

To get to the city, I cycle from home and then take a train. One morning I rushed to the station on my bike and ran on to the platform, relieved to find the train was running late. I joked with the lady next to me about how often I am grateful for the times it runs late. I then had a conversation with her and she revealed to me how important it is for Christians to lift up their eyes and actually see the people around them. She told me of an occasion when she had experienced exactly that: someone noticing her during some major heartache. She told me about some of the loss and pain she had gone through and said that one day she had been feeling so sad and alone when she was in a car park packing her groceries into the boot of the car after doing her shopping. A complete stranger approached her and asked why she looked so sad. She was taken by surprise, but nonetheless proceeded to pour out her heart, grateful for someone who was prepared to listen. Afterwards the stranger offered to pray for her, which she accepted. "She said some lovely kind words over me and I felt strengthened," explained the lady as we sat on the train. This incident had had a profound effect on this woman and helped her considerably. I then shared with her that part of my job was to encourage Christians to *look out* for those around them and to engage with them about their faith. For this lady who had told me her story this looking out and engaging was the best thing that could have happened to her; it proved to be something of a life-changing meeting when a complete stranger in a car park prayed for her. I felt honoured to have heard that story.

As we approached the final station the lady thanked me for listening. I shared some words of the love of God and encouraged her to pop in to one of her local churches. She told me how good it had been to talk, but, to be honest, I felt I was the one who had received something valuable. I thanked the lady for sharing a snippet of her life with me.

Too often we miss the opportunities that Jesus gives to us to be his hands and feet, by assuming that someone else will do it. Someone else will reach out to the groups of young people in my village, or those on the streets late at night. Someone else will visit the elderly in the care homes, someone else will welcome the new families who have recently moved into our community, someone else will take assemblies and pray for the schools, or become a street pastor or pray for the sick in the village. The list could go on and on.

One of my favourite episodes of *The Simpsons* is when, after the bin-men refuse to collect his refuse because he calls them "trash eating scum bags", Homer takes on the Springfield Council rubbish collection service. He runs for the job of sanitation commissioner and through various shenanigans is elected. It is a landslide victory on the strength of his slogan: "Can't someone else do it?" Once elected, he hires an army of rubbish collectors who not only literally take rubbish out of homes, round the clock, but also do the most bizarre cleaning jobs like changing nappies, mopping up spilt beer and helping members of the rock band U2 pull up their trousers when their bum-cracks are showing! (If you haven't seen the episode, this doesn't seem so bizarre on the screen!) For me, this cartoon illustrates a point: in reply to the great commission, the western church, on the whole, has responded passively: "Can't someone else do it?" In reply to the great commission to "go into all the world and preach the good news to all of creation" (Mark 16:15), we have either sent specialist teams or overly eager young Christians, while the majority of the church chooses to remain inactive, like a sleeping giant, impotent and disobedient. The order to reach the world has been heard, yet we allow the world to remain unreached. In these end times, the whole church is required; we need the diverse gifts and the breadth and depth of all the church to reach out to this fallen world and to offer hope in Jesus' name.

Nowhere have I witnessed the "Can't someone else do it?" response so painfully and clearly as when I recently taught a seminar on sharing faith. Around 50 people turned up and I thought I had spoken passionately about loving people and always being prepared to give the reason for the hope that we have. I pleaded with those at the meeting to do something to bring the good news of Jesus to those who haven't got a clue about him. I must admit I was on a bit of a preaching roll when I was rudely interrupted by the banging of the door and a man walking in off the street. I stopped what I was saying and welcomed him in, showing him where he could sit down - near the front by the area where, in five minutes' time, people from other seminars would stream in for their coffee break. He was sent by heaven. Here in our midst was an example of the kind of person we should all reach out to. Poor soul, the odds were 50-1 against him! He had walked into a session on evangelism, and I felt rather sorry for him as I anticipated how the zealous participants would spring on him!

The man sat and listened patiently until the end of the session as I spoke about letting people know the good news of Jesus. I finished by offering to pray with those who wanted the boldness to share in this way - and a number of people responded. As I prayed with these people I was distracted, because I had one eye on the man who had walked in. He was sitting alone and ignored. 50 people walked past this man who had meandered into the session and sat down in front of us all. Not a single delegate greeted him, let alone asked him if he was all right or would like a cup of tea. It wasn't as if they might have assumed he was another delegate; it was painfully obvious that he wasn't. He didn't have a name badge on for a start!

I apologised to the lady to whom I was talking and explained that I was thinking about the man who had come in off the streets. I went up to him, asked if he was all right and offered him a cup of tea. He declined the drink, but began to talk about how he was doing and to let me know about some struggles he was having. He explained that he had come into the church building because he needed help. He needed to talk to someone. We sat and spoke together for a while and I offered to pray for him which he gratefully accepted. "Thank you for listening," he said as he went out of the door that he had gingerly pushed open an hour previously. I enjoyed meeting that man and listening to him talk about his life, worries and heartache and how much he longed to amend his ways. While it was a privilege to have met him, I so wish that one or two out of the 50 people who had been to my sharing faith seminar had truly noticed him walk in. Perhaps they might have engaged with him, but I honestly believe that no one actually saw him; somehow they missed him. We need to take our "can't someone else do it?" spectacles off and start seeing people as loved by God and valuable and to see our encounters with them as divinely planned, not merely down to chance.

Jesus admonished his disciples when they asked why he talked to a woman at a well in Samaria: "Open your eyes and look at the fields." (John 4:35) Other versions state: "Lift up your eyes." (NKJV) The Message puts it like this: "Open your eyes and take a good look at what's right in front of you." I believe that God is calling us to open our eyes, to lift them away from ourselves and our circumstances and begin to see people as valuable, somehow divinely brought to us so that we can share what we have. This certainly doesn't mean launching in with a full-fat message of what it means to be a Christian. Rather we are called to see that people are able to receive and to have what we have. It may be that we connect with people in the simplest way, like the complete stranger who asked the woman whom I met on the train why she was so sad. For me, I always ask people whom I engage with how they are doing, or, if they are people working behind a counter, I ask how their day is going. Most of the time people are happy to talk. If we reach out to people and take an interest in them then the opportunities to bring something of our faith to people will arise naturally.

Big-Hearted evangelism is a participatory activity

I reckon you must know by now that doing evangelism isn't just about presenting a message or theme in the vague hope that some people may be able to understand what we are saying. Believe it or not, I still meet Christians who are incredibly frustrated with the response they get from doing evangelism. They have (in their understanding) shared it and no one seems the slightest bit interested in what they have to say. There's a little ditty I have held on to all my life as a Christian that I am glad to share with you: "Good news needs to be understood as good news, otherwise it's no news, which is bad news." No matter how good the message, it is only good if it is perceived as such. The gospel contextualised so that others can understand and begin to engage with it is a powerful thing. The gospel presented in a way that no one can comprehend, isn't.

Much of what I seek to do as a street evangelist welcomes people to question the various art pieces or visual aids, if they want to. For example, The Light Project has over the years set up a free shoe shine in city centres for the day or afternoon. When people sit and have their shoes cleaned for free, they often ask why. "We are re-enacting an old story of a man who washed the feet of his friends. We can't wash feet on the streets, so we are shining shoes instead!" Most people ask: "Who was that man?" Other examples are when I use visual art installations which are constructed from doors and gates or I give away fresh bread or bottles of water. People want to know more. I usually give some explanation, but not much, and I base it upon the *once upon a time* opening of a traditional story. So I say, "Once upon a time there was a man who said, 'I am the Gate.'..." or, "Once upon a time there was a man who said, 'Look, I am standing at the door and knocking.'..." or "Once upon a time there was a man who said, 'I am the bread of life.'..." Most people want to know who that man was and why he would make such strange statements about himself.

Another way I encourage people to question, is simply by showing something of the story of Jesus and then letting them try to work it out. Christmas is a good opportunity for these kinds of questioning stories. One year, I placed a baby doll, dressed in white clothes, to represent Jesus in a beautiful manger, and then surrounded it with piles of rubbish. Amongst the rubbish was a small sign: "God became a man." While some people thought the scene had been vandalised by young people throwing rubbish at it, others studied it and some said, "Ah, now I get it..."

Another year, a week before Christmas Day, I set up an empty travel cot and had three security guards stand by it for the morning. People looked in astonishment. "Why are you three guarding an empty cot?" people queried. "The king is coming," was the reply. Most people then looked even more shocked: "What? Here in this city? A king?" The guards gently explained that, by Christmas Day, they were sure a king would have been born. It was at that point most people understood, but some didn't. Then the guards gave even more information, "We've heard the king is going to be called Jesus!"

Allowing people to question what we do isn't just for a street scene, but for our whole lives. Peter teaches us that we should always be geared up to give an answer for the reason for the hope that we have. (1 Peter 3:15) I wrote this poem as a prayer that people would question why I do what I do:

Questioned Christian

I want to be a questioned Christian,
A provoke hope type of one
Not a pain in the neck, annoying or a sigh as I walk in the room,
But a spark off questions follower, a "tell me the answer" walker

I long to be a questioned Christian,
That others would ask me for the reasons,

Those who despair all around me, broken, bruised, battered by life's journey may seek the one who oozes healing balm through the hope that dwells deep down, flowing from the core of my very being.

I long to be a questioned Christian,
Geared up, prepared, not ashamed to say or cover it up kind of one.
But to reveal the untameable, unimaginable, despite the heartache-able,

So I want to be a questioned Christian,
A ready, steady, go, on your marks, get set, run kind of one,
Filled with a new strength, to simply tell the reason for the hope that I am.

Being willing to allow people to participate in what we do by asking questions isn't the sum total of evangelism that is participatory. We need to be willing to allow others to *have a go*. My colleague Glyn Jones who heads up The Light Project in Chester has done some refreshing work and study on this very issue. You may think that to do participatory evangelism is to invite others to belong before they believe. Glyn believes this notion is flawed and argues that the recent across the denominations attempts to invite people to church should really be termed "attend before you believe" as they appear to secure the spectatorship of seekers, rather than actively incorporating them. Here are some examples of what Glyn has done to try to work out what participative evangelism may look like:

- A community fun-day which is run and hosted by the church, but staffed by the local community members
- Evangelistic theatre, where the participants are non-church attendees
- Beer and Carols night in a struggling community pub

He also has run an evangelism course for non-Christians inspired by the TV documentary series on Channel 4, "Make Me a Christian". (2009) Glyn writes: "In this course, participants are presented with the basics of Christian faith and asked to consider and discuss them, as with many popular evangelism courses. In addition to this, they are also asked to take part in the working life of the church, including its mission and evangelism, work in a homeless shelter, varied Christian worship and a piece of street theatre as well as corporate prayer. The hope was that they would actually grasp faith better if they took part in its very expression themselves. Such approaches, grounded in experiential learning allow people not only to learn in different ways, but encourage commitment and belonging rather than just learning."[44]

My own experience in this kind of evangelism isn't as well developed as Glyn's, but nonetheless I have been inspired by his work and have sought to emulate what he seeks to do in allowing others an opportunity to try out and experience what it means to be a Christian. I was umming and ahing what to do one afternoon when my wife sent me out of the house with the instructions to "go and tell people about Jesus" in the city of Peterborough. "Give out some bottles of water," she suggested cheerfully. "You're good at that!"

I left reluctantly, feeling a bit lonely as I had recently moved to a new area and was missing my team. I'm so pleased I did go as I caught a glimpse of our big-hearted God; his plans in the midst of my feeble efforts unfolded right before me. But it wasn't easy - for me. When I arrived in the city centre, since I was feeling nervous and because I was worried about how people, in a strange city I didn't know, would take to someone like me, handing out free bottles of water with a big "free water" sign and wearing a t-shirt that asked "Thirsty?" in an overly-friendly font. I procrastinated. So I went to pray. On this occasion, it really was an excuse to do nothing. I chose an empty bit of space on the Cathedral Green and felt quite justified in interceding while tucking into a prawn sandwich. At least I did, until I was very rudely interrupted by a group of girls who sat near me and spoke very loudly - about sex. Their intrusive rude conversation made me get off my backside and go and actually do something. As I left my cosy prayer meeting for one I said to myself: "I hope I don't see *those* kind of girls when I do my street evangelism." Well, you've guessed it, after 10 minutes of handing out bottles of water and talking with people, the very same group of girls sauntered down the road towards me. They didn't pass me by, but chose to gather around to ask lots of questions about what I was doing. I tried to explain, in the most off-putting way, that I was offering free bottles of water to let people know something of the free gift of Jesus. I explained that Jesus said that if anyone was thirsty they should come to him. Their response astonished me as, one by one, they asked if they could help! So, I had a choice, and for some bizarre reason I said, "Yes please, that would be great." These girls were the most incredible help; they looked after all my stuff when I went to get more water and ice because we soon ran out due to quite a buzz around my free water give-away. Groups of lads gathered around, initially attracted to the pretty girls, and only then to notice the not-so pretty guy giving away free bottles of water and to hear about the man who declared that he was the water of life. A small group of young men and woman stayed with me for the afternoon and we spoke together about Jesus and life. It was then that I received the most amazing compliment from a young person I have ever had. The guy simply said: "I wish our RE Teacher at school was like you, we could learn something about God." The small group of young people agreed. So, either their RE teacher was a right idiot and by comparison I came off quite well, or, for some of those young people, they connected with something of the good news of Jesus.

However, the story doesn't stop there. Four months later and I am on the streets jollying people into our "Get in the Picture" Christmas project, which is housed in a disused shop. A team serve tea and coffee and mince pies, as well as offering people the chance to take part in the nativity scene and have their picture taken. On this afternoon, a group of young people came in and I recognised one of the girls. Later on, as they were leaving the shop, this young lady tells me that she has recently become a Christian and joined a local church. "I helped give out bottles of water," she smiles.

This is a happy story. Yet my attempts to include people in what I do haven't always been a success, and at times I have regretted asking people to help me to do evangelism. Once, when I painted a massive six by six foot painting of a cross, I left the paints and brushes in the hands of a man I had only met earlier that day. He wasn't a Christian, but enjoyed taking part in the painting and learning something of the good news in the process. While I was doing a street performance, another man vandalised my painting with some creative writing which made mums who passed by cover the eyes of their children. The guy whom I had left in charge of the paints gently said to the man that he couldn't do that, it wasn't allowed. However, he didn't listen and the creative swear painting carried on. So my trusted helper punched him in the face. That's not such a good example of participative evangelism.

Yet, allowing people to question what we do and making it easier for people to participate in the Christian life are big-hearted ways of engaging with others with something of the good news of Jesus. We can develop this further. Working with other partnerships in the community, such as shopping centre staff and people of other faiths, can be an amazing opportunity to show and tell the gospel. Street Pastors has had a phenomenal success in many towns and cities up and down the United Kingdom, as well as internationally, through fostering positive partnerships between the church, the local council and the police. They call it the Urban Trinity. This, they argue, is about working together for the betterment of communities. This positive engagement is a challenge for those of us who long to see more and more people get to grips with the good news, yet only want to rely on our own resources. I hope that if you think like that, you may be inspired to see evangelism as less of an *us* and *them* activity and rather one which we can do alongside others and with people who are not Christians.

Jesus tells us we need to be like children to enter the Kingdom of God. My youngest daughter, Milly, is incredibly positive. When she was three we used to cycle back from nursery and sometimes we would take the route that passes a big cemetery and crematorium. Instead of looking at the grey drab stones and monuments, all she saw were the flowers. "Look, Daddy, flowers!" she would announce. "More flowers!" One time she saw some oil in the road after there had been some rain. "Look, Daddy! A rainbow!" She makes me smile.

Like Milly, we need to look at things differently when it comes to evangelism and deciding whom we can work with in it and whom we can't. We need to look at partnerships with those who are not Christians as positive and as an opportunity to show and tell something of the gospel. Too often I meet groups of Christians who resist working with people, rather than being confident that they can glory in something which can affect and inspire others as they work with them. Too often we can be fearful: "The gospel will be watered down ... They won't understand what we want to do ... Our hands will be tied and we won't be able to speak about Jesus." These are concerns I have heard over the years from different groups of Christians as we have tried to work together positively with others in our community. My best buddy, Jon Phillips, who is now training to be a pioneer minister, used to head up all of the community youth projects for The Light Project. I heard him explain once to the Head of the Council Youth Services that if they wanted to give us money for equipment then they needed to be clear that we would talk to the young people about Jesus. They were somewhat surprised by the forthright nature of Jon's convictions, but still bent over backwards to give some funding for the youth work and partner with us. We need to look at things differently while being true to our own convictions.

I was with a group of Church leaders once, praying for a particular city. Some of my fellow ministers were in shock about the word "Pride", which the council had chosen to represent the city. We were led in a worried time of prayer, a time of real concern for the city with the word "pride" over it. As I too spent time praying about that word, I couldn't help but smile and a few cheeky giggles could be heard from my corner of the room. The word had been chosen to encourage tourism and trade within the city and I was picturing Jesus walking around with a big chunky marker, going up to signs with the word "Pride" on them and with one little half circle graffiti swipe changing "Pride" to "Bride". This picture of Jesus helped me to pray; every time I saw the word "pride" in association with the city it served as a reminder that Jesus is proud of his people and that many more will be added to the body of Christ, becoming the most beautiful bride.

Recently I had coffee with a guy who looks after the public side of things in a large shopping centre. I arranged the meeting to ask whether the churches would be able to use some space inside it at Christmas to share something of the nativity story. "We can't seem to welcome one particular religious group into the shopping centre over another," he told me. I understood and explained that if we were given any space we would be sensitive to those around us and be gentle in how we shared the Christmas story. However, things were not looking hopeful. As the meeting was wrapping up, he mentioned the thought of arranging a flash mob in the shopping centre at Christmas which could be put on YouTube. "Great idea!" I enthused and shared with him about a flash mob that I had seen online, where choirs started singing The Hallelujah Chorus from Handel's Messiah. "That's exactly what we want!" he exclaimed eagerly. "Can you arrange it?" So, I had to take stock. Gently and quietly talking to people about the Christmas story and putting on some fun Christmas activities was a no-no. But singing out praises to Jesus as loudly as we could with as many people as I could muster was a big yes! Working in partnership with others sometimes takes me by surprise.

BIG HEARTED

CONCLUSION

Doing Big-Hearted Evangelism is about being integral with who we are

I believe God made me for a purpose, but he also made me fast.
And when I run I feel His pleasure.
Attributed to Eric Liddell, from the film "Chariots of Fire"

To conclude this book I want to present to you the idea that to be big-hearted we must be true to ourselves. If we are not true to how God has gifted us and how he has wonderfully made us, being big-hearted is really hard.

I am a street evangelist, not for the kick of having a wacky career, but because I love people and it's on the streets I encounter lots of them. I also recognise, through this love for people, that I need to do something about the fact that the majority of them do not have a clue about the best news ever. So I spend time on the streets communicating by using the gifts I have got, and I use them with great delight.

Some of the ideas and creativity that I have outlined may resonate with you and you may want to use them to connect with others. But primarily, I hope you see my heart in why I do what I do, rather than just the things in and of themselves. Simon is a pastor with a huge heart to do things differently for the sake of his community. You may long for what Simon has done. For him it was a step-by- step journey with the church, which was at times painful. It wasn't an overnight decision to become Re:New. I hope you also see his heart through his stories and that you desire to be led by God to have a big-hearted church like him, but your journey will look very different to his.

So, without wanting to undo our passionate plea to be big-hearted people, the message is simple: if you haven't done so already, use your *own* gifts in showing something of the big-heartedness of the God whom we serve. By all means, take our ideas and use them, but better still apply what you've got.

Copying people just doesn't work. I know because I've tried. It has left me frustrated at times and feeling somewhat lost and, besides, it requires too much effort to keep up the pretence. I'm not very good at pretending and I usually get found out. So, trying to be all sensible and clever just doesn't work for me! Time and time again, I'm asked to speak at events and meetings that require a tie and some smart trousers. Yet my engagement with people still doesn't change much. I've tried to do it differently and I become a stammering wreck. It's only when I am true to who I am, share some stories and heart-felt convictions that people seem to get what I'm going on about, and I have a good time too in the process.

Please know that big-hearted evangelism is deep and broad and isn't done in just one way. If every person in our nation is going to encounter something of the good news of Jesus, then it will take all our efforts in lots of novel and fresh ways to reach them. We, I believe, are in an age where we all need to use what we have got to reach out. We need to use dance, the arts, media, writing, clowning, poetry and theatre. These are some of the ways we can use what we have proudly to show-off our Jesus.

The fact that evangelism isn't done in just one or two ways I hope will be good news for you. You see, evangelism as a pitch, patter or presentation just leaves creative people feeling cold. To be imaginative in how we demonstrate our faith brings me delight and I seem to learn so much in the process. I recently did an art project using clay on a council housing estate in Birmingham - Chelmsley Wood. It wasn't something I just decided to do randomly, it was planned, as I have an unusual role as an artist in residence, doing loads of different art pieces, as part of a creative mission project called "Tree of Life".

The idea behind this imaginative venture is to engage with people who haven't got a clue about the Christian story; to talk and engage on spiritual matters and in so doing to encourage people to join in and explore what it means to be a follower of Jesus. So, it's less of a watch and observe kind of art project and more of a hands on kind of thing, allowing others to experience the Christian faith while doing creative things and, I hope, learning something about Jesus in the process. Yet, on this particular clay art occasion, it was me who had the revelation.

You see, my pot making art piece just went all wrong. It started well when I encouraged as many people as possible to make pots with me and in so doing to contribute to the sculpture. Young and old joined in, as well as some very inquisitive, bored teenagers who had noticed the "FREE POT" sign, pointing to the Baptist church; they had failed to read the smaller word "making" beneath. After a whole day making pots with people, I had around 80 different ones. I asked a question of everyone who joined me: "Is your glass half full or half empty?" I then gently explained that it needn't be one or the other. Rather, through resources that are beyond us, I spoke about our cup overflowing, quoting the often used Psalm 23 to describe what God is like and the kind of care he has for us. For some, the idea that their lives could overflow, was music to their ears.

I took the pots home to dry out before firing them in the kiln, but, much to my horror, after a few days every single one of them had cracked or broken in the drying process. I decided that I would have to fix all 80. Then, not having the time to do a great big fix up, I went for the option of just using what I had. It was then that I felt God reveal to me something most profound: despite and because of my brokenness, my cup overflows. I felt humbled. My original intention to produce something water-tight and aesthetically beautiful now seemed to have a far greater meaning. You see, we are able to have lives in abundance, refreshed and vibrant, because of the one who is like a river living in us, and he seeps out through our brokenness and fragility. When I set up the sculpture in the community for others to appreciate, this seemed to connect with people far more than if the pots had been whole and sturdy.

However, engaging with art can be a much simpler exercise than making lots of pots! One art student I worked with on the streets came up with a borrowed idea, where she had heard of a guy who uses chalk on the pavement to talk with others and ask God to turn up by his Spirit to heal people. I just so happened to have a pile of chalks with me for some street outreach, but didn't know what to do with them! My friend took them and went off with another team member and started to draw pictures and then started to draw stars, like the ones you see on the pavement in Hollywood. Only she called these destiny stars; she welcomed people to step on them and then she wrote their name and spoke words that God gave her for them. I watched for a while and saw how it connected with people; many listened and responded. It was so simple, yet it worked so well. A piece of chalk worth two pence brought direction and much valued comfort to many people who dared to venture on to a star drawn simply on the pavement.

One of our Light Project students wanted to show people who attended our Night Church (an outreach to clubbers late into the night) what it meant to be part of the body of Christ. She made lots of cakes, but left out different ingredients for each one. The cakes looked pitiful, a right mess. Only the one with all the right ingredients looked tasty and cake-like. She called her art installation: "divided we fall". It spoke powerfully to the team members running Night Church, as well as to the guests who turned up.

Please, take hold of these simple stories as proof that you have permission to do what God has gifted you to do to reach this world! This plea of mine, I believe is vital for the sake of those who have yet to feel and hear what we have as followers of Christ. We have to move on from the idea that evangelism is done by the expert, who is the evangelist. In the past it has been the evangelist who has been some kind of spiritual salesman, able to close the deal and have the confidence to proclaim the gospel. Today, we need all of us to show creatively and cleverly the wonderful message of Jesus through our gifts and abilities. Ken Robinson describes this process of using our creativity and applying it as the "Element", a meeting point between natural aptitude and personal passion. He observes that, when people do the things they love with their gifting, it is in that place that they find their most authentic selves. Time seems to pass differently and in the place of 'element' people are more alive, more centred, and more vibrant.[45]

This principle of being in our element is for the well-being and sanity of Christians, as well as a means to communicate and show the gospel very differently to those around us who may have a big mix of learning styles. There is no one way in which all people will be able to understand the good news of Jesus. People are different and will get the gospel differently. We need reminding of this truth and to be aware that we can too often fall back into a mindset that it's one size fits all when it comes to faith sharing. Paul writes, "I have become all things to all people so that by all possible means I might save some." (1 Corinthians 9:22) Why is it we can often behave as if we have become a *few* things for *some* people, who just so happen to be the intellectuals, who enjoy debating and arguing the case for or against the Christian faith or those who are well-educated, who can handle long lectures on the Christian faith?

In the pub last night I spoke with my friend who isn't a Christian about how nervous I felt when in prison speaking to a group of young men. I had some cool stories and fun wacky activities, yet the butterflies raged in my ample tummy as I stood in front of the group and the prison staff. I wanted them to get it and to connect with the simple stories and to see how the Bible teaching linked with the theme. I tried to speak in a language that would make sense, using words of youth culture and I was careful not to use unnecessary jargon. You see, most people just don't get the story of God in the words that we are so accustomed to; creative means are needed to communicate - it is vital for the survival of the Christian faith. I believe we are in a season of permission. It's not a case of anything goes for the sake of it, but rather one of lavish creativity and communication which allows people to say: "Ah, now I get it!" My friend thought my grappling with how the message can be communicated was hilarious, so I used a load of Christianese and jargon to see how he got on with what I was trying to say. He looked dumbfounded at my gobbledegook. My point was made.

Your call to change this world for Jesus will be unique. We are called differently to do radical things for God that may seem strange, but it's not for our ego or something that will only appeal to our intellect. God will call you to use what you have got. Let me give an example of two dear friends of mine in France who have a unique call. Philippe and Veronique Gatti are inspirational. Since I'm in the business of bringing the news of Jesus to as many people as possible and in ways that people can connect with so that in time they may choose to become followers of Jesus, the Gattis inspire me to keep going when times are tough. We first met nine years ago in Chester, when they came to work with me and the growing Light Project team and to learn English too. They joined me on the streets feeding the hungry and helping the homeless. They also worked in some of the youth projects.

Since then, they have dedicated their lives to bringing the gospel to people in remote places, including Peru and Nepal, and have also done a few treks in Europe. One was a 99 day hike from the South of France to Switzerland along the Alps, a journey of just under 1,000 kilometers. They met around 600 people who asked for information about their trek and who were chuffed to receive a copy of Mark's gospel and a story about why they were embarking on a walk in remote places.

They prayed with people and spent time listening too. Recently I asked whether their feet and legs ached after their long walk. Phil said no, but then pointed to his ears. He explained that these hurt from hearing hundreds of stories as people poured out their hearts on encountering two adventurers for Jesus, willing to be there, available for Jesus to use. They take the initiative, respond to their unique calling and gifting and seek to play their part in pointing people to our big-hearted God.

I believe we need to do unique and new things. Without us taking action, people just won't get an opportunity to connect with and enjoy the gospel message. Many of our trusted tools are broken and those that remain are just too few. We need breadth and depth. We need new ideas and initiatives that break free from the fear of getting dirty if we hang out with those who are not part of our groups or usual middle class culture.

Our prayer for you is that you will now commit to following Jesus in being big-hearted. Not just an activity now and again, but a day-to-day following after him. We hope this adventure of following takes you to new places, as you can't really follow Jesus into more nice church meetings or comfy familiarity, as he doesn't tend to venture there much.

We hope you may follow him where he goes. Scripture shows us that he dares to step out eagerly to seek those who are bruised, battered and broken. We follow Jesus to the lost, as they are on his horizon. We walk in his slipstream and come face to face with those who lack hope and are in need of love, as they are his focus.

BIG HEARTED

Take a few minutes to imagine what your city, town or village would look like if each one of us woke up every morning with an ache of the heart of a hurting Father and asked to which place and to whom we could bring his big-heart. It blows me away that the lavish healing balm of the Spirit is drenched upon captured minds and freedom breaks out for those who have sat in darkness all their lives ... through us. This is humbling, that our Big-Hearted Father has chosen to reveal his love, through me and you.

References

[1] Jim Currin, *Sharing Faith The Jesus Way*, BRF (2011) p.66 Used with permission

[2] Glen Marshall, contribution to *Beyond 400: Baptists imagining life after 400 years* – "17. A theological, religious, sectarian, worldly, modest, bold and nuanced future" Used with permission

[3] See Nazir- Ali M, *From Everywhere to Everywhere,* Collins Flame (1990) p.170 for a further explanation on God's heart for the poor

[4] Wallis J, *The Soul Of Politics* Mariner Books (1994) p.164 Used with permission

[5] Jim Currin, *Sharing Faith The Jesus Way*, BRF (2011) p. 67 Used with permission

[6] Baptist Union of Great Britain, *Five Core Values for a Gospel People*, Baptist Union of Great Britain (1996) Used with permission

[7] Brother Thomas of Celano, *The First Life of St. Francis*, (1230) from paragraph 23 (Chapter x)

[8] Brother Thomas of Celano, *ibid*, paraphrases of paragraphs 22 and 23 (Chapters ix and x)

[9] Cray, G. et al, *Mission-Shaped Church*, Church House (2004) Used with permission

[10] Cray, G. et al, *ibid*, p.xii Used with permission

[11] Murray, S., *Church After Christendom*, Paternoster (2004) p.7 Used with permission

[12] Ashworth, J. & Farthing, I., *Churchgoing in the UK*, Tear Fund (2007) p.7 Used with permission

[13] Ashworth, J. & Farthing, I., *ibid*, p.7 Used with permission

[14] John 12:24-25 (TNIV) The words in verse 25 are also found in Matthew 10:39 and 16:25, Mark 8:35, Luke 9:24 and Luke 17:33

[15] Cray, G et al *op. cit.* p.89 Used with permission

[16] The Archbishops' Council, *Common Worship*, Church House Publishing (2000) p.xi Used with permission

[17] Saint Bonaventure, *Life of St. Francis of Assisi*, (1263) paraphrase of the first paragraph of chapter 2

[18] Hebrews 10:20 and the preceding two chapters

[19] Matthew 27:51; Mark 15:38; Luke 23:45

[20] 1 Corinthians 3:16; 1 Corinthians 6:19; 1 Peter 2:5

[21] Acts 13:14-43; Acts 14:1; Acts 17:1-3, 10-12, 17; Acts 18:4-5, 19; Acts 19:8-10

[22] See, for example, Philemon 1:2

[23] Saint Bonaventure, *op. cit.*, paraphrase of the first two paragraphs of chapter 2

[24] This story can be found in all four gospels: Matthew 14:14-21, Mark 6:35-44, Luke 9:12-17, John 6:5-13

[25] 2 Corinthians 8-9

[26] 2 Corinthians 8:15, a reference to Exodus 16:18

[27] Lynne Twist, *The Soul of Money: Transforming your Relationship with Money and Life*, W.W. Norton & Co., (2003) pp.102-3 Used with permission

[28] Brother Thomas of Celano , *op. cit*, paraphrases of paragraph 17 (chapter vii)

[29] Brother Ugolino, *The Little Flowers of St. Francis of Assisi*, (c1390) paraphrase of a selection from chapter xxv

[30] James Strong, *Exhaustive Concordance of the Bible*, Hendrickson (1894) G5485

[31] Richard Thomas, *Counting People In: Changing The Way We Think About Membership And The Church*, SPCK (2003), pp.53-54 Used with permission

[32] "The Story of Cottenham" can be found at http://www.cngt.org.uk/new_page_6.htm , the website of the Church Network for Gypsies and Travellers (accessed on 10 May 2011) Used with permission

[33] One example of such a complaint is found in Matthew 9:11 (NIV)

[34] See for example the stories of the woman caught in adultery, John 8:3-11, and the woman at the well, John 4:4-29

[35] Brother Thomas of Celano, *op. cit*, paraphrase of a selection from paragraph 72 (chapter xxvii)

[36] "Dave Vaughan on Big Brother", at http://www.crossrhythms.co.uk/articles/life/Dave_Vaughan_On_Big_Brother/41736/p1/ (accessed on 11 May 2011) gives a transcript of the interview between Sarah J of Cross Rhythms and Dave Vaughan and was published on the website on 1 October 2010 Used with permission

[37] Baptist Union of Great Britain, *op.cit.* p.14 Used with permission

[38] Luke 11:9-10

[39] 2 Corinthians 12:9

[40] Aliss Cresswell *A Diary of Miracles*, Pickard Communication (2010) Used with permission

[41] A sermon by Tony Campolo "The Big-Hearted Christian" Programme number 4422 First broadcast 4 March 2001 on *30 Good Minutes*, produced by the Chicago Sunday Evening Club www.30goodminutes.org. Used with permission

[42] John Drane, *Celebrity Culture*, Rutherford House (2005) p. 83 Used with permission

[43] As an aside, I love how the Spirit calls Peter, "Simon"; his birth name. The name God has always known him by. In spite of being called Peter for over four or so years, first by Jesus, and then be everyone else, the Spirit calls him "Simon". It makes me think about the importance of intimacy with God even thought we may be in

ministry and have great responsibility. To hear our name being called by God is vital for us.

44 Glyn Jones, *Evangelism and Evangelicalism*, The Light Project. Used with permission

45 This book is fascinating. It challenges me to see how evangelism needs to be connected with our gifts and passion. I hope and pray that we will see more artists rise up to do what they were made to do to share the good news of Jesus. Ken Robinson, *The Element: How Finding your Passion Changes Everything,* Penguin (2010)

Chris Duffett has also written Smack Heads and Fat Cats:

For more information visit
www.gileadbookspublishing.com/smack-heads-and-fat-cats
or scan the following QR code: